RESURRECTING YOUR DREAM

Everyone Had a Dream... What Happened to Yours?

Scot C. Moore

ISBN: 979-8-9955642-0-1

Contents

Introduction

The Morning Your Dream Got Up

There's something about early morning—the quiet space between darkness and dawn—when the world feels uncertain and possibility still lingers in the air. It's the hour when yesterday hasn't fully released its grip and tomorrow hasn't yet announced itself. The world is still, almost sacred, as if the earth itself is holding its breath.

The story begins there.

A few women walked toward a tomb before sunrise, carrying spices for burial and the weight of disappointment in their hearts. They were not coming with expectation; they were coming with responsibility. They were doing what you do when you believe something is over—showing up to honor what used to be and preparing to make peace with a loss you didn't choose.

In their minds, the stone was still sealed.

The grave was still final.

The story was still finished.

But when they arrived, they found the unexpected.

The stone had already been rolled away.

The silence of death had been interrupted by the sound of hope. And in that single moment, they discovered a truth that continues to echo through the lives of ordinary people:

What looks like the end is sometimes the doorway into a new beginning.

That moment recorded in Luke's Gospel is more than a story of resurrection. It is a picture of how life often works.

All of us, at some point, stand before something we believed was finished—a relationship, a dream, a vision, a goal, even a version of ourselves—and we feel that familiar mix of heartbreak and disbelief. We show up ready to bury what used to be. We bring our own "spices"—explanations, rationalizations, coping mechanisms—anything that helps us accept what feels permanently gone.

And yet, sometimes life surprises us.

God surprises us.

Hope surprises us.

Because there are moments when what we thought was dead has simply been waiting for the right morning to rise again.

Maybe that's where you are right now.

Once upon a time, you had a dream. A clear vision of who you wanted to be, what you wanted to build, and how you wanted your life to matter. But somewhere along the way, disappointment crept in. Delay stretched longer than you expected. Responsibilities grew heavier. Reality grew louder.

Before you realized it, you stopped dreaming—not in one dramatic decision, but quietly, gradually, almost politely.

You didn't mean to stop.

It just happened.

You buried your dream beneath bills, failures, fatigue, fear, or the slow grind of survival. You told yourself, "Maybe that was just a phase." But deep down, something inside you still stirs—a whisper that refuses to die, a pulse beneath the surface, a quiet longing that shows up when you are alone with your thoughts.

That whisper is not accidental.

It is a reminder.

Your dream may be buried, but it is not gone.

And that is what this book is about.

It is about rediscovering that whisper—the one that reminds you your dream is not dead, only hidden beneath the weight of life. It is about brushing off what you left behind and daring to believe that the same power that brings light to a dark morning can breathe life back into the parts of you that went silent.

You don't have to be a pastor or preacher to understand resurrection.

Anyone who has ever stood up after being knocked down…

rebuilt after being broken…

or started again after losing everything…

You understand resurrection.

It is the quiet courage to believe again.

It is the decision to rise when you have every reason to stay down.

It is choosing possibility when pain would be easier.

Yes, I am a pastor—and I believe in the God who still rolls stones away. But even if you don't consider yourself religious, you have likely felt the pull of that same divine energy: the force that turns endings into beginnings, pain into purpose, and obstacles into opportunities.

Call it faith.

Call it resilience.

Call it grace.

Call it grit.

Whatever name you give it, resurrection is the comeback story written into the human soul.

In the chapters ahead, we will walk through the process of bringing your dream back to life. We will face the Fridays of life—the painful seasons of loss and letting go. We will sit in the long Saturdays—those quiet seasons of waiting when nothing seems to move. And together we will celebrate the Sundays—the breakthrough moments when purpose begins to breathe again.

You are holding this book for a reason.

You may have buried your dream, but your dream has not buried you.

Something inside you is still alive.

Still calling.

Still reaching for the light.

And as you turn these pages, I pray you will discover what those women found on that quiet morning long ago:

The stone has already been rolled away.

What you thought was over may just be beginning again.

Because your dream isn't dead.

It's waiting for you to believe again.

Author's Note

Before You Turn the Page.

I've always believed that everyone carries a dream.

Not the kind that fades when the alarm clock rings, but the kind that wakes you up in the first place—the quiet vision of who you were meant to be and how your life might make a difference.

But life has a way of testing what we believe.

Responsibilities grow heavier.

Disappointments accumulate.

Reality gets loud.

And sometimes, without even realizing it, we stop dreaming.

I know what that feels like.

There were seasons in my own life when I stood at what felt like the grave of something I once believed God had placed inside me. The passion was still there, but the momentum was gone. The calling was real, but the circumstances felt overwhelming. And like many people who love God deeply, I found myself asking a quiet question:

Can this live again?

This book was born in that tension.

Not from a place of easy triumph, but from the honest journey of rediscovering hope when dreams feel distant. I wrote these pages for people who still believe in God but sometimes struggle to believe in themselves. For people who feel called to something greater but find themselves tired from the climb.

Resurrecting Your Dream is not simply a collection of sermons or inspirational ideas. It is a journey—through the hard places, through the waiting seasons, and ultimately back to hope.

It is for anyone who has ever felt like their dream died while they were still alive.

Before you read another page, I want you to hear this clearly:

You are not too old.

It is not too late.

And God is not finished.

Your dream may have been delayed.

It may have taken a detour.

It may even look buried.

But delay is not denial, and endings are often disguised beginnings.

So as you read this book, give yourself permission to believe again.

Read slowly.

Reflect honestly.

Pay attention to the places where God may still be speaking to your heart.

Because the same power that raised hope from a tomb is still breathing life into people today.

I wrote this book for the dreamers who fell asleep, the believers who got bruised, and the builders who grew tired.

I wrote it for those who are still trying—and for those who stopped trying a long time ago.

Most of all, I wrote it for you.

Welcome to your resurrection.

— Rev. Scot C. Moore

Senior Pastor, Judah Temple A.M.E. Zion Church

Mitchellville, Maryland

Stop Settling For Saturday

There's a moment in life that feels like standing in an elevator between floors—suspended, waiting, wondering when movement will return. The lights flicker. You hit buttons that don't respond. You check your reflection in the stainless-steel door and think, *This wasn't supposed to happen here.* That's Saturday.

We love to talk about Friday and Sunday. Friday was the day of loss, pain, and the cross. Sunday was the day of victory, resurrection, and power. But Saturday is where we spend most of our lives—somewhere between the trauma of what happened and the triumph of what's coming next. Saturday is the day that doesn't get a lot of preaching, because Saturday doesn't feel like a testimony. It feels like a question.

The Space Between What Was and What Will Be

The women who loved Jesus showed up to the tomb with spices to anoint His body. They expected sorrow. They didn't expect resurrection. And that's what Saturday does—it conditions us to expect the same pain tomorrow that we experienced yesterday. It trains us to anticipate disappointment and call it wisdom.

Saturday is the place between promise and performance, calling and completion, dream and destiny. It's the in-between space where you wrestle with the silence of God and the noise of your doubts. Maybe you've been there—when the job closed, the relationship ended, the business collapsed, the diagnosis came back, or the plan fell apart. You know what God said, but you can't reconcile it with what you see. That's Saturday. It's the day you whisper, *I thought I'd be further by now.*

The disciples lived that moment. They had left everything to follow Jesus. They believed He would lead them into victory, but by Friday night, all their dreams were buried with Him. On Saturday, they hid—scattered, confused, and heartbroken. Hope felt heavy. Faith felt foolish. And yet, even though Saturday felt like the end, it was really the pause before the power.

The Failure of Friday Isn't Final

Friday was brutal. There's no point in pretending otherwise. It hurt to watch something so full of promise fall apart. But failure does not mean finality. The death of one dream can become the doorway to another.

I've sat with people in their Fridays—marriages that collapsed, businesses that went bankrupt, people who buried loved ones and thought they buried their purpose with them. In one of those conversations, an old friend reached out after losing his daughter. He said, "Man, I just knew if I could talk to you, maybe something would make sense." We cried, we talked, we prayed. He was living through his Friday. But even in that dark space, I reminded him, "Friday isn't forever."

That's the first truth of resurrection life: the failure of Friday is never the finale of faith. David said, "Yea, though I walk through the valley of the shadow of death…" He didn't say, "to the valley." He said, "through." That means there's movement, even in the middle. The valley may slow you down, but it cannot stop you. If you can still breathe, you can still believe.

So whatever your Friday was—the breakup, the betrayal, the layoff, the loss—it might have buried your expectations, but it didn't bury your existence. You're still here. And if you're still here, Sunday is still possible.

Saturday: The Silent Struggle

If Friday is pain and Sunday is power, Saturday is processing. It's the day of "nothing." The day that looks unproductive but is actually preparational. Think of a seed. Before it breaks ground, it breaks open. And that breaking happens in the dark. You don't see it. You can't measure it. You just wait.

When I was a kid, we planted seeds in Styrofoam cups for a science project. After three days, nothing had sprouted. I told my mother, "My seed is broken." She smiled and said, "Be patient. Just because you can't see it doesn't mean nothing's happening."

That's the mystery of Saturday. It's the day that looks empty but is actually full of invisible movement. Something is happening—in the dark, under the surface, beyond your awareness. And if you can learn to honor what's happening underground, you won't panic just because you can't point to progress above ground.

Settling in the Space Called "Okay"

The danger of Saturday isn't despair—it's comfort. You survived Friday. You made it through the storm. You learned how to function again. And now, you've built a routine around survival. It's not terrible. It's just okay.

But Jesus didn't die for okay. He didn't rise so we could maintain mediocrity. He rose so we could walk in resurrection power.

"Okay" is safe, but it's also stagnant. It's predictable. It requires no faith, no risk, no courage. It's waking up to the same schedule, the same habits, the same hopes, and calling it peace—when really, it's paralysis.

Here's what I've learned: comfort can become captivity. The longer you stay in Saturday, the harder it becomes to move toward Sunday. And the longer you call mediocrity "normal," the more abnormal purpose begins to feel.

So let me ask: have you settled? Have you accepted half of what God promised because you were tired of being disappointed by the other half? Have you built a home in the waiting room instead of the destination?

When Life Feels Like It's Between Floors

I remember being trapped in an elevator once. It stopped between floors—nowhere near where I wanted to be. I pressed the button. Nothing happened. Finally, I picked up the phone to call for help. The man on the other end said, "Don't worry, the elevator's just resetting. Once it's done, you'll be able to go higher."

That word hit my spirit. Sometimes, when it feels like life has stopped, it's not breaking down—it's resetting. The system is recalibrating. You're not being punished; you're being prepared for a higher floor.

A reset isn't comfortable. It's quiet. It's uncertain. But it's necessary. You can't ascend until the system aligns. You can't rise until the inner work is complete. Maybe the delay you're experiencing isn't denial—it's design. Maybe God is using Saturday to stabilize what would collapse under the weight of Sunday.

When God Stirs Your Saturday

There's a pattern that repeats throughout Scripture: when people settle too long, God stirs things up. Israel settled in comfort, and captivity came to shake them back to purpose. The same happens to us. We call it frustration, but God calls it forward.

When you won't move, He'll send movement to you—not to destroy you, but to develop you. The breakup that pushed you to pray. The layoff that forced you to innovate. The silence that made you seek. That's not random—that's resurrection training.

The Power of Sunday

Only a few ever make it to Sunday. It's not because Sunday is exclusive, but because Sunday requires expectation. Sunday requires faith that what you buried can breathe again.

When Jesus rose, He declared, "All power is given unto Me." That same power now lives within you—power to create, to forgive, to rebuild, to believe again. The Spirit of God doesn't only make you spiritual—it makes you strong, strategic, and steady. It's not just for tongues and tears. It's for tough decisions, daily battles, and divine assignments.

The resurrection isn't just about life after death. It's about life after disappointment.

The Stone Was Rolled Away — For You

When the women arrived at the tomb, the stone was already rolled away. Not because Jesus needed a path out, but because they needed a path in. Sometimes God moves the obstacle not to release Him, but to reveal the truth to you: it's already done.

The stone moved so they could see the evidence of resurrection. And maybe God is rolling stones in your life right now—things that once blocked your view, now shifting so you can finally see what He's been doing all along.

From Wakanda to the Word

If you've seen *Black Panther*, you remember that scene.

The throne room is tense. The ritual combat has begun. T'Challa and Killmonger circle each other. It's not just a fight for position—it's a fight for identity, for legacy, for the future of Wakanda. The drums beat. The crowd watches. The ancestors are invoked.

And then the unthinkable happens.

Killmonger overpowers him. He lifts him. And throws him over the waterfall.

You can hear the gasps. You can feel the shock. The king falls into the mist below, swallowed by water and stone. The throne is seized. The crown is taken. Wakanda moves on as if it's over.

That's Friday.

That's the moment when what you thought would last collapses. When the position you prayed for slips through your hands. When the vision you carried feels like it died in public.

But here's what the camera shows us next.

T'Challa is not dead.

Another tribe—the Jabari—finds him in the cold. Broken. Wounded. Frozen in the snow. They don't parade him. They don't announce him. They don't post it. They hide him.

They tend to his wounds.

They wrap him in warmth.

They guard him while he heals.

That's Saturday.

Saturday is not dramatic. Saturday is quiet. Saturday is hidden. Saturday is recovery without applause. Saturday is when God keeps you alive in the cold while everyone else assumes you're finished.

Saturday is where pride is stripped. Where perspective is reshaped. Where strength is rebuilt beneath the surface.

And then comes the moment.

The moment when T'Challa stands again.

The moment when he walks back into the throne room—not as the man who fell, but as the man who survived. He doesn't return angry. He returns anchored. He doesn't reclaim the throne out of revenge, but out of responsibility.

That's Sunday.

That's resurrection.

And here's the spiritual truth in the story:

What looked like death was only interruption.

What looked like defeat was only development.

What looked like the end was only hidden preparation.

You can throw purpose off a cliff—but you cannot kill it.

You can bury destiny—but you cannot cancel it.

Because if God ordained it, even your fall becomes part of the formation.

Some of you have had waterfall moments.

Public losses.

Private heartbreaks.

Dreams that felt like they were stripped from your hands.

But if you're still breathing, you're still in Saturday—not finished.

And Saturday is not burial.

Saturday is buffering.

Saturday is where God preserves what He plans to restore.

Because you can't kill purpose.

You can only bury it temporarily.

And when God says it's time—

You will rise.

Rooted Before Rising

The palm tree stands tall because its roots grow deep. It bends but doesn't break because it was built in the dark. Before any plant reaches upward, it reaches downward. Saturday is root work. It's the unseen development that sustains visible success.

You might not see growth yet, but something's happening underground. Every prayer, every tear, every decision not to quit—they're all roots strengthening your future.

Closing Thought

Saturday is not a sentence—it's a stage. It's not punishment—it's preparation. Don't unpack your bags in the waiting room. Something is happening in the dark. And when your Sunday comes—because it will—you'll see that the tomb was never your end. It was just the beginning of your comeback.

Reflection

Be honest about your Fridays. What in your life has ended, failed, or fallen apart? Name it without minimizing it, because naming pain is the first step toward healing. Then look at your Saturday routines—where have you settled for survival instead of pursuing growth? What "good enough" has replaced "God's best"?

As you write, consider whether God might be resetting you. Where might He be stabilizing you, strengthening you, or deepening your roots before you rise again? Finally, choose one small Sunday step— one act of faith that moves you forward: write the plan, make the call, try again.

Before you close this chapter, speak life over your dream: *Friday didn't finish me. Saturday won't stop me. Sunday is still coming.*

Declaration

I declare that Saturday is not my destination.

I declare that what looks like a pause is often preparation.

I refuse to settle for "okay" when God has promised "more."

I will keep believing in the middle.

I will keep growing in the dark.

I will take one faithful step at a time.

Sunday is still coming for me.

Prayer

God, thank You that even in the middle You are working. Thank You that failure isn't final, that silence doesn't mean absence, and that every seed in the dark is growing toward the light. Help me not to settle in the safe spaces of "okay." Reset me, strengthen me, and prepare me for resurrection. In Jesus' name, Amen.

Dreaming in the Dark

When Vision Outruns Visibility

Darkness has always had a way of unsettling us. It blurs the familiar, magnifies uncertainty, and tempts us to believe that nothing good can happen when we can't see what's in front of us. Yet, paradoxically, some of the most transformative work God performs in our lives happens in the dark. Before anything grows, it begins in obscurity. Before clarity comes conviction. Before light comes learning. Before revelation comes wrestling.

Joseph's journey illustrates this truth in vivid detail.

He didn't step into his dream through celebration. He stepped into it through a conspiracy.

Scripture tells us that when Joseph was approaching his brothers from a distance, they said to one another, *"Here comes this dreamer."* They didn't mean it as a compliment. His dream irritated them. His potential provoked them. His future exposed their insecurity. So they plotted against him — not because of who he was, but because of what he carried.

And that's often the experience of dreamers: your dream doesn't always bring applause. Sometimes it attracts attack.

Before Joseph could even greet his brothers, they stripped him of the coat his father gave him — the symbol of favor, identity, and belonging — and threw him into a deep, dark pit. Not metaphorical darkness, but real, suffocating, sight-stealing darkness. A place where he couldn't climb out, couldn't see escape, couldn't understand why this was happening, and couldn't hear anything except the echo of voices discussing what would become of his dream.

Most people would have assumed the dream died right there.

But that's the paradox of dreaming in the dark:

Sometimes your dream is not dying — it's developing.

When Disruption Becomes the Delivery Room of Destiny

Dreams rarely unfold without disruption. We imagine success as a straight line, but God often draws our destiny with detours. The very moment Joseph received his dream, his life became more complicated. His brothers misunderstood him, his journey was interrupted, and the ground beneath him shifted.

But disruption is not destruction.

Sometimes disruption is divine.

We pray for elevation, but don't always pray for the process required to sustain elevation. Dreams are never delivered in sterile environments. They come through the chaos of change, the discomfort of growth, and the unpredictability of life.

Like gold refined by fire, Joseph's dream required heat. It required friction. It required a setting so uncomfortable that Joseph had to rely on God in ways he never imagined. The pit was not a punishment — it was part of the preparation.

And that's true for us, too. Some dreamers are shaped most deeply in the seasons that make the least sense. We don't always recognize it at the time, but God is using the very thing that frightened us to form us.

The Gift of Darkness

Joseph's pit wasn't just deep — it was dark.

And the darkness was disorienting.

It wasn't simply the physical depth of the cistern that shook him. It was the sudden loss of orientation. One moment he was standing in daylight, wrapped in a coat that symbolized promise. The next moment he was stripped, shoved, and swallowed by shadow.

Darkness does something to your equilibrium.

When the lights go out, your confidence wavers. You reach for walls that aren't where you thought they were. You extend your hands cautiously. You move slower. You listen harder. You feel more vulnerable.

And that is precisely why darkness terrifies us.

It removes our sense of control.

In the light, we strategize.

In the light, we measure progress.

In the light, we plan.

But in the dark, we surrender.

We can't chart our way forward.

We can't see what's ahead.

We can't predict the next step.

But here is the paradox: darkness doesn't just conceal — it reveals.

It reveals what we truly trust.

It reveals where our confidence actually rests.

It reveals how dependent we are on what we can see.

Light gives us information.

Darkness gives us formation.

Ask someone who has lost their sight how they navigate the world, and they will tell you something profound: when one sense fades, the others sharpen.

Hearing becomes more precise.

Touch becomes more sensitive.

Awareness becomes heightened.

They learn to "see" differently.

And that is exactly what happens spiritually in dark seasons.

When God turns the lights out, He fine-tunes your ability to hear Him.

Faith is not built by sight; faith is built by sound.

"Faith comes by hearing…" (Romans 10:17).

Notice the order: hearing first — then believing.

When Joseph was in the pit, he could not see the palace.

He could not see Potiphar's house.

He could not see the prison.

He could not see Pharaoh's court.

All he had was what God had already spoken.

And sometimes God will reduce your vision so He can increase your hearing.

Because as long as we can see clearly, we tend to lean on ourselves.

But when clarity disappears, dependency develops.

Dark seasons strip away distraction.

They quiet the noise.

They remove applause.

They silence comparison.

And in that silence, you begin to detect the whisper.

The whisper that says:

"I am still with you."

"This is not the end."

"I am shaping you."

"Stay steady."

Perhaps that's why God allows us to pass through seasons where clarity vanishes — seasons where the map disappears and the only thing left is trust.

Because trust is stronger than sight.

Sight can deceive you.

Sight can intimidate you.

Sight can overwhelm you.

But the voice of God anchors you.

Joseph's darkness was not abandonment — it was adjustment.

God was recalibrating him.

Before Joseph could lead a nation, he had to learn to hear beyond emotion. Before he could manage abundance, he had to survive scarcity. Before he could interpret dreams for Pharaoh, he had to hold onto his own dream in silence.

God is not absent in the dark.

He is active in ways you cannot detect.

He is strengthening your spiritual senses.

He is increasing your internal stability.

He is teaching you how to walk by faith, not by sight.

And here is the mercy in it:

If God exposed you too early, the light would blind you.

If He elevated you too quickly, the spotlight would distort you.

If He answered you too fast, you might mistake His gift for your ability.

So sometimes He dims the lights — not to harm you, but to harden you in the right way.

The dark is not punishment.

It is preparation.

It is the sacred space where confidence in self fades and confidence in God forms.

And when the lights come back on — and they will — you will not emerge desperate for validation.

You will emerge steady.

Because what is developed in darkness can survive in daylight.

The Hidden Work Beneath the Surface

If Joseph's pit teaches us anything, it's this: darkness is not the end — it is the incubator of destiny.

When his brothers stripped him of his coat and dropped him into that dry cistern, it looked like interruption. It looked like betrayal. It looked like the death of a dream spoken too boldly. The sky above him grew smaller as he sank into the earth. Voices that once called him brother now faded into the distance.

But what Joseph did not know — and what we often do not realize — is that the pit was not cancellation. It was concealment.

Because every significant creation God makes begins in the dark.

A seed does not begin in sunlight. It begins underground, surrounded by pressure, soil, and silence. From the outside, it looks buried. But beneath the surface, roots are stretching, systems are forming, life is organizing itself in unseen ways. Before it ever breaks through the surface, it has already grown downward.

A baby does not begin in a nursery. It begins in the hidden sanctuary of a womb. No applause. No audience. Just formation. Cells multiplying. Organs developing. A heartbeat forming in secret before it ever echoes in the open air.

A diamond does not sparkle in the sky. It is compressed deep within the earth. Heat. Pressure. Time. It becomes brilliant not because it avoided darkness, but because it endured it.

Even a photograph — something meant to capture light — must first pass through a darkroom.

Darkness is not evidence that God is distant.

Darkness is evidence that God is deliberate.

When I was in college, working as an amateur photographer, I learned something that changed the way I view seasons of obscurity. After taking a picture, you don't immediately expose it to light. You take the film into a darkroom. You close the door. You work quietly. You immerse it in solution. You wait.

You don't rush the process.

You don't flip on the lights prematurely.

Because too much light at the wrong moment erases the image.

Exposure before development ruins the outcome.

And that's how God handles us.

He protects the dream by hiding it while He shapes it — and shapes us — in private.

Joseph's pit was a darkroom.

Potiphar's house was a darkroom.

The prison cell was a darkroom.

Each stage looked like delay, but each stage was development.

The dream God gave him at seventeen needed a backbone that could handle a palace at thirty. It needed maturity. It needed humility. It needed resilience. It needed the kind of character that can manage power without being consumed by it.

You cannot rule what you have not been refined to steward.

Some people look at their lives and say, "I'm buried."

But buried and planted look identical from the outside.

The difference is in what happens next.

Buried means forgotten.

Planted means positioned.

Buried means the story is over.

Planted means growth is underway.

If God planted you, you are not done growing.

Something is happening beneath the surface.

Conversations are shaping you.

Pressure is strengthening you.

Silence is sharpening you.

Delay is deepening you.

And just because nobody sees it does not mean nothing is happening.

Joseph's brothers thought they ended him.

But they accidentally positioned him.

Because the pit was not the end of the dream.

It was the first step toward the palace.

So if you're in a dark season right now — if you feel unseen, overlooked, or forgotten — don't panic.

Darkness is not denial.

It is incubation.

And when God decides the time is right, what was hidden will rise — not fragile, but fortified.

Not immature, but intentional.

Not weak, but ready.

Because what God develops in the dark can withstand the light.

Destiny Decisions Are Made in the Dark

Joseph's future wasn't determined in the palace. It wasn't decided when he interpreted Pharaoh's dream or when he rose to power. It wasn't sealed when he wore the robe of authority.

Joseph's destiny was decided in the pit.

It was in the darkness — stripped, alone, betrayed — that God began positioning him for the palace. Long before Joseph saw the fulfillment of his dream, God was arranging every detail to lead him exactly where he needed to go.

We often think destiny forms in moments of celebration, clarity, and confidence. But more often, destiny is forged in the quiet, unseen, uncomfortable places where our character is shaped, our faith is stretched, and our identity is refined.

A baby is unaware of the world outside the womb, yet everything that world requires is being formed in the dark.

A seed doesn't know how tall it will grow, but its roots are strengthened in the soil long before it ever breaks through the surface.

A diamond has no idea how valuable it is becoming; it only knows pressure.

So it is with dreamers.

What God is forming in you in the dark will sustain you in the light.

Learning to Walk by Faith, Not Sight

Darkness does something else — it trains us to move differently.

A blind man develops a different relationship with movement. He navigates not by what he sees, but by what he senses. He learns to trust touch, sound, memory, and instinct. He learns to trust something beyond sight.

Christians are called to do the same.

Scripture says, *"We walk by faith, not by sight."*

The problem is, most of us want to walk by faith while still relying on sight to make the first move. But darkness removes the illusion of control. It forces us to trust God's voice, God's leading, God's timing.

It forces us to lean into hearing more than seeing.

No wonder the enemy attacks your hearing — because hearing is what builds your faith.

You don't need light to become stronger.

You need trust.

And darkness is where trust is strengthened.

The Rhythm of Night and Morning

In the Hebrew understanding of time, a day does not begin with morning.

It begins with evening.

"And the evening and the morning were the first day."

To God, darkness is not the end of a day — it is the beginning of one.

Nightfall does not signal decline. Nightfall signals development.

Night is not a dismissal — it is preparation.

Joy comes in the morning, but the work of joy begins at midnight.

When you feel surrounded by darkness, God may not be closing your story — He may be starting a new chapter.

What Looks Like Burial May Be Planting

When Joseph was thrown into the pit, everyone assumed that was the end of the story. His brothers walked away believing they had eliminated the dreamer. But God was using the very moment of darkness as the turning point of his destiny.

That's the beauty of God's process:

He does His best work in places that look like endings.

Joseph was not buried — he was planted.

And dreamers planted in the dark always rise again.

Conclusion: The Dream Is Not Dead — It's Developing

If you find yourself in a pit-like season — confused, stripped, isolated, or unsure — don't misinterpret the moment. Darkness is not a sign of God's absence; it is often the evidence of God's activity.

Joseph didn't know it, but the pit positioned him for a palace he had never imagined.

You may not realize it now, but the dark place you're in may be developing something in you that the light could never produce.

Your dream is still alive.

It has not died.

It has not disappeared.

It is being formed, refined, and prepared for its reveal.

You are not being punished.

You are being prepared.

And when morning comes — because it will — you'll discover what every dreamer eventually learns:

Dreamers don't die in the dark.

Dreamers develop in the dark.

Dreamers rise from the dark.

And your rise is coming.

A Mother's Dream

Scripture Focus: 2 Kings 4:8–37 (NKJV excerpts)

"Let us make a small upper room on the wall… a bed, a table, a chair, and a lampstand…" (v.10)

"About this time next year you shall embrace a son." (v.16)

"Is it well with you? … And she answered, 'It is well.'" (vv.26)

"…the child sneezed seven times, and the child opened his eyes." (v.35)

Life has a way of leading us right to the edge of something new and uncertain—and then asking a question we'd rather avoid: *Do you trust Me?* Not when the path is paved and predictable, but when it's invisible and uncomfortable. That's where faith lives—between what was and what will be.

It's the same question Aladdin asked Jasmine as he reached out his hand and invited her onto that magic carpet. She had never seen anything like it. No rails, no logic, no control—just a carpet suspended in the air and a boy saying, "Do you trust me?" That's the moment between comfort and calling, between fear and faith. She had to decide whether to step into something she didn't understand, simply because the invitation felt right.

God asks us the same question. Do you trust Me enough to step into something you've never seen before? Even when tears still streak your cheeks. Even when your heart is tired from disappointment. Even when the next move makes no sense.

That's exactly where the Shunammite woman found herself. We don't know her name — just her posture of faith. She's a woman with means but with missing pieces; successful but still searching. Her story begins in the mundane, when a traveling prophet named Elisha passes through her town. She recognizes something sacred in him, and in a moment of divine discernment, she decides to make room for what she doesn't yet understand. And that's where everything changes.

Room for the Holy: Preparing Before You Possess

Before there was a promise, there was preparation. "Let's build a small room…" she said to her husband. Not for comfort, but for connection. She wasn't chasing a miracle — she was creating space for God. That's what real faith does. It builds a bed before there's a guest, sets a table before there's a meal, lights a lamp before there's a word.

Her hospitality became holy architecture — an act of spiritual construction that said to heaven, *You are welcome here.*

We often want to receive the promise before we prepare for it, but faith flips the order. Noah built an ark before rain. The Shunammite built an upper room before conception. Preparation is prophecy in action. Every nail she hammered was a declaration: *I believe God is coming this way again.*

And God did. Elisha asked, "What can be done for you?" She didn't request anything. But Gehazi noticed the silent ache: "She has no son, and her husband is old." The prophet spoke the unspoken dream: "About this time next year, you will hold a son."

Her first reaction was pain disguised as caution: *Please, man of God, don't mislead your servant.* Translation: Don't wake the hope I buried years ago.

But God specializes in reviving what we stopped believing in. And sure enough, "The woman became pregnant… and gave birth to a son, just as Elisha had said."

Guarding the Promise: Words That War for What God Spoke

The story turns quickly. The boy grew, went out to the fields, cried, "My head, my head!"—and by noon, he was dead. Just that fast, her long-awaited dream became her greatest heartbreak.

But what she did next separates her from most. She didn't call for mourners. She didn't plan a funeral. She carried the boy upstairs— to the very room she built for God—and laid him on the bed of the prophet. Then she shut the door and went out. She didn't lay him in the grave; she laid him in God's presence.

Her husband questioned her urgency. Her answer was simple: "It is well." Those words were not denial—they were defiant faith. She refused to give the enemy the satisfaction of hearing her doubt. Faith doesn't always shout; sometimes it simply refuses to agree with fear.

Even when Gehazi ran ahead with the staff, nothing happened. Because sometimes the resource is not enough—you need the Source. The prophet himself came, shut the door, prayed, stretched out—mouth to mouth, eyes to eyes, hands to hands—walked, prayed again, stretched again, and suddenly the child sneezed seven times and opened his eyes.

God is so precise that even the sneezes preached. Seven—the number of completion—a divine exhale that announced: *The process is finished.*

Staying with God: Perseverance That Refuses to Let Go

When Elisha first sent Gehazi ahead with his staff, the Shunammite woman did not move.

She did not argue loudly.

She did not create a scene.

She simply made a decision.

"As surely as the Lord lives and as you live, I will not leave you."

That statement is not dramatic — it is determined.

She had already carried her dead son to the prophet's room. She had already laid him on the bed that she built in faith. She had already traveled miles with grief in her chest and questions in her mind. And now the prophet sends his servant instead of coming himself.

For many of us, that would have been enough to discourage us.

But perseverance speaks differently.

She was not disrespecting Gehazi.

She was discerning divine proximity.

She knew this: the presence matters.

And she refused to detach from the one carrying the anointing.

That is the heartbeat of perseverance.

Perseverance is not loud.

It is loyal.

It is the kind of faith that says, "I don't understand this process, but I'm not leaving God."

It is the kind of resolve that says, "I will not disconnect from the source, even if the answer hasn't arrived."

We often define perseverance as waiting.

But perseverance is more than waiting.

It is staying.

Staying when you don't see progress.

Staying when you don't feel God.

Staying when the promise feels fragile.

Staying when others suggest it's time to move on.

There are moments when logic says, "Accept it."

When emotion says, "Detach."

When pain says, "Protect yourself."

But faith says, "Stay."

Faith is not always about giant leaps over mountains.

Sometimes it is about quiet loyalty in the valley.

Sometimes it is about waking up and saying, "God, I'm still here."

The Shunammite woman refused to let go of divine presence, even when the process was confusing.

And that kind of perseverance changes outcomes.

Because presence carries power.

We see the same stubborn faith in the woman with the issue of blood.

Twelve years of suffering.

Twelve years of doctors.

Twelve years of disappointment.

She had every reason to quit. Every reason to withdraw. Every reason to isolate.

According to the law, she was unclean.

According to culture, she was disqualified.

According to medicine, she was hopeless.

But faith does something extraordinary when everything else has failed.

She pressed.

The crowd was thick. The space was tight. The path was blocked.

But when the upper path is blocked, faith goes lower.

She crawled.

She reached.

She touched the hem.

And that touch was not casual — it was courageous.

She wasn't grabbing fabric. She was grabbing promise.

She wasn't touching cloth. She was touching covenant.

And the text says immediately — immediately — power flowed.

Notice something powerful here: she didn't wait for Jesus to stop. She didn't wait for the crowd to clear. She didn't wait for someone to escort her forward.

She pressed through discomfort.

She persevered through resistance.

She refused to let go of the possibility that God could still move.

Breakthrough often belongs to those who stay when staying feels foolish.

Who press when pressing feels exhausting.

Who reach when reaching feels risky.

The Shunammite woman stayed with Elisha.

The woman with the issue of blood pressed toward Jesus.

And both stories teach us something essential:

Perseverance is proximity.

It is refusing to let distance grow between you and God.

It is holding on when it would be easier to release.

It is saying, "I may not understand this season, but I will not disconnect from the One who controls it."

There are seasons when faith looks glamorous.

And there are seasons when faith looks like grit.

Faith sometimes looks like worship with tears in your eyes.

Sometimes it looks like prayer without answers.

Sometimes it looks like showing up again when you're tired of showing up.

But perseverance refuses to let grief become goodbye.

It refuses to let delay become departure.

It refuses to let confusion become separation.

And here is the truth that anchors it all:

God honors staying.

Not because He needs your loyalty — but because staying positions you for resurrection.

The Shunammite woman's miracle did not happen at the first instruction.

It happened because she stayed.

And sometimes the difference between loss and restoration is not God's ability — it is our refusal to walk away.

Why the Details Matter

Every detail in this story preaches. The upper room reminds us that preparation precedes presence. The bed, table, chair, and lamp speak to rest, revelation, authority, and illumination—an environment for encounter. The shut door teaches boundaries. The seven sneezes declare completion. God doesn't restore halfway; He restores fully.

And for every mother—and everyone who "mothers" a vision—this story is a mirror. You may not be raising a child, but you are carrying something: a ministry, a business, a community, a calling. This chapter honors everyone who has ever nurtured something divine and dared to believe again after disappointment.

Reflection

What "upper room" do you need to create—in time, space, or focus—to make room for what God wants to do next? Where do you need to change your confession from panic to prophecy? Write your "It is well" for this season.

What dream have you stopped believing for, and how might God be asking you to lay it back in His presence again—back on the bed where it belongs? Who are your "Gehazis" (helpful but limited), and where do you need to seek the Source instead of relying only on resources? Finally, write one act of perseverance you can take this week—one decision that says, *I will not leave until it lives.*

Declaration

I make room for God.

I guard what God has given.

I will not leave until it lives.

It is well.

Prayer

God, thank You for being the Keeper of my dreams. Teach me to prepare a place for Your presence, to protect what You've spoken, and to persevere through the process. Where I've buried hope, breathe on it again. Where I've stopped believing, stir me to try again. I trust You with the parts of my story that still feel unfinished. You are still the God who resurrects. In Jesus' name, Amen.

Delay is Not Denial

Scripture Focus: Habakkuk 2:2-4

There comes a point in every dreamer's journey when obedience has already happened, faith has already been exercised, and prayer has already been offered—yet nothing seems to be moving. This is the space between promise and fulfillment, the place where belief is no longer inspirational but necessary. It is here that many dreams quietly begin to fade, not because God stopped speaking, but because waiting became heavier than expected.

This chapter speaks directly to that space.

If Chapter one challenged us to stop settling for Saturday, and Chapter two taught us how to keep dreaming in the dark, and Chapter three reminded us that some dreams require preparation, protection, and perseverance, then this chapter addresses what often follows obedience: delay. Not denial. Delay.

Habakkuk knew this space well. He had heard from God, yet what he saw around him did not match what he had been promised. He prayed, questioned, and waited. And when God finally responded, He did not offer a timeline or a detailed explanation. Instead, He gave Habakkuk instructions.

"Write the vision and make it plain on tablets, that he may run who reads it. For the vision is yet for an appointed time… though it tarries, wait for it; because it will surely come, it will not tarry."

In *The Message* translation, God's words feel deeply personal. He tells Habakkuk to write what he sees, to make it bold and clear, because the vision itself is leaning toward the future. It aches to come to pass. It is not lying. If it seems slow, wait—because it is on its way and will arrive right on time.

That language matters. Delay often convinces us that nothing is happening, when in reality something is being prepared. God is not silent—He is strategic.

When Waiting Feels Like Rejection

Most believers do not struggle with God's ability.

We struggle with God's pace.

We believe He can do it.

We just wonder why He hasn't.

Delay has a way of whispering lies — subtle ones.

Not loud accusations.

Not obvious rebellion.

Just quiet suggestions.

"Maybe it wasn't for you."

"Maybe you misunderstood."

"Maybe you missed your window."

"Maybe it's too late now."

Delay does not usually attack your theology.

It attacks your timing.

It makes you measure yourself against calendars instead of calling.

We live in a culture obsessed with acceleration. Thirty under thirty. Forty under forty. Viral by morning. Successful by sunset. If you are not early, you are assumed to be late.

But heaven does not operate on social media timelines.

God is not intimidated by your birthday.

Yet many people quietly assume dreams are only for the young. That there is a shelf life on vision. That somehow time has disqualified them.

But dreams do not have expiration dates.

People do.

And the only thing that truly expires a dream is surrender.

History quietly contradicts the lie that it is "too late."

Christian Dior did not rise early in life. He did not become the name that reshaped fashion until later. Colonel Sanders was well past what society would consider his "prime years" when his chicken recipe finally gained traction. He was turned down repeatedly — not once, not twice, but over and over again. Yet the world now consumes what he refused to abandon.

The irony is that many people who dismiss late starts are still enjoying the results of someone else's perseverance.

You may be sitting in a building designed by someone who succeeded late.

Eating at a restaurant founded by someone who was once rejected.

Wearing clothes inspired by someone who was overlooked.

If age did not stop you from benefiting from their dream, do not let age stop you from pursuing your own.

But waiting does more than challenge our confidence — it exposes our insecurities.

When the dream tarries, we begin to internalize silence as rejection.

We say things like:

"Maybe God chose someone else."

"Maybe I'm not gifted enough."

"Maybe I don't have what it takes."

And slowly, delay begins to feel personal.

But here is the theological correction:

God's delay is not divine rejection.

It is divine calibration.

Habakkuk says, "Though the vision tarries, wait for it; because it will surely come, it will not tarry."

That sounds contradictory at first — it tarries, but it will not tarry.

What it means is this: it may feel slow to you, but it is not slow to God.

God does not rush preparation.

Because what you receive too early, you may mishandle.

What you step into prematurely, you may sabotage.

Time does not weaken a true dream.

It tests it.

And what survives testing becomes stronger.

Waiting feels like rejection when we mistake process for punishment.

But often, what feels like a closed door is simply God adjusting the room.

Joseph waited.

Abraham waited.

Moses waited.

David waited.

Jesus waited thirty years before beginning three.

Delay is not evidence of disqualification.

It is evidence of development.

There are things God must form in you before He fulfills through you.

Character before platform.

Depth before visibility.

Stability before expansion.

And sometimes, the only reason it feels like rejection is because you assumed completion would come sooner.

But God is not obligated to move at the speed of your expectation.

He moves at the pace of your preparation.

Delay is not denial.

It is timing.

It is the quiet assurance that when it does arrive, you will be ready — not just to receive it, but to sustain it.

And if the dream is still alive in your heart, that alone is evidence it has not expired.

Because God does not tease His children.

He develops them.

So if you are waiting, do not interpret the silence as rejection.

Interpret it as refinement.

Because what God promises, He fulfills — not when you are impatient, but when you are prepared.

Delayed Is Not the Same as Canceled

One of the clearest lessons about delay comes from something as ordinary as air travel. Anyone who flies regularly knows the feeling. You rush to pack, rush to get to the airport, rush through security — only to look up and see the word *delayed* glowing on the board. It feels frustrating and unnecessary, especially when you did everything right.

But there is a crucial difference between delayed and canceled.

A delayed flight still reaches its destination — it just arrives later than expected.

I experienced this firsthand while traveling to New York. With everything happening in the news about flights, nerves were already high. Sure enough, the flight was delayed. I did not arrive when I planned, but I still arrived. And in a way only God can orchestrate, that delay allowed the person picking me up to pick up another traveler at the same time. What felt inconvenient for me became coordinated for someone else.

Sometimes your delay has little to do with you. Sometimes God is aligning people, timing, and circumstances in ways you cannot see. What feels like wasted time may actually be divine synchronization.

That is why God tells Habakkuk the vision has an appointed time. Appointments are intentional. Heaven has already scheduled what earth has not yet revealed.

Clarity Before Completion

God's first instruction in Habakkuk is not to wait — it is to write.

That alone disrupts how most of us approach dreams.

We want manifestation before documentation.

We want completion before clarification.

We want movement before meaning.

But God says, "Write the vision."

Writing forces clarity.

You can carry a feeling for years.

You can carry inspiration for decades.

But until you define it, you cannot direct it.

Inspiration without clarity leads to frustration.

You can be excited and still be ineffective.

You can be passionate and still be scattered.

Writing requires you to wrestle with what you actually believe God said.

It forces you to move the dream from emotion to articulation.

From impression to intention.

From vague desire to visible direction.

God gives vision — but He expects you to work through the details.

That was certainly true when we began building Judah Temple.

God did not drop a finished blueprint from heaven.

He did not specify the number of chairs.

He did not dictate the height of the stage.

He did not email a diagram for camera placement.

He gave vision.

And then He gave responsibility.

There is a difference between revelation and construction.

Revelation tells you what could be.

Construction demands you decide how it will be.

I remember sitting with an architect during the early planning stages. After discussing measurements and possibilities, he paused and asked a simple, but profound question:

"What do you see?"

Not what do you hope.

Not what do you wish.

Not what do you think is affordable.

What do you see?

Vision always begins with sight.

Not natural sight — spiritual sight.

And in that moment, I had to articulate what I had been carrying internally.

I described the flow of the room.

The feel of the worship space.

The way people would enter.

The atmosphere we believed would be cultivated there.

As I described what I saw, he began to sketch.

At first, it was just lines on paper.

Rough outlines.

Basic shapes.

But over time, those sketches became renderings.

Those renderings became plans.

Those plans became permits.

Those permits became walls.

Those walls became a sanctuary.

What people now walk into and worship in started as clarity on paper.

We had to see it before others could see it.

We had to write it before we could build it.

And here is the truth: if we had not defined it, it would have remained a dream in conversation instead of a structure in reality.

Clarity precedes completion.

Walt Disney understood this principle long before Mickey Mouse became a global icon.

Before there was Disneyland.

Before there were theme parks.

Before there was cultural dominance.

There were sketches.

There were storyboards.

There were drawings people laughed at.

When Disney pitched his ideas, bankers called them unrealistic. Critics called them childish. Investors hesitated. Others saw a mouse.

He saw a world.

He saw characters.

He saw parks.

He saw experiences.

Clarity allowed him to hold onto what did not yet exist.

He wasn't clinging to fantasy.

He was stewarding vision.

And vision that is clearly defined becomes resilient against ridicule.

But clarity also requires wisdom.

Not everyone should have access to your dream.

Some people call themselves realists when, in truth, they are limiters.

They do not see constraints as challenges to overcome — they see them as reasons to stop.

They have never built anything large, so everything sounds impossible.

They have never stretched, so expansion sounds irresponsible.

Dreams should be shared with people who will pray, encourage, and help refine — not diminish.

Refinement strengthens vision.

Reduction suffocates it.

Even Joseph learned this lesson the hard way. He shared his dream with brothers who lacked capacity to celebrate it. Not everyone is ready to handle what God has shown you.

Discernment protects destiny.

Most people do not lose their dreams.

They lose sight of them.

Life crowds vision.

Bills distract attention.

Criticism shakes confidence.

Delay blurs clarity.

And when clarity fades, courage weakens.

That is why dreamers keep reminders close.

They revisit what God said — not because they doubt Him, but because clarity strengthens courage.

They reread the journal.

They revisit the notes.

They pray over the original word.

They redraw the sketch.

Because writing anchors what waiting tests.

Completion may take time.

But clarity gives you something to hold onto while you wait.

And if you can keep seeing it clearly — even when you cannot see it physically — you are already closer to completion than you think.

Waiting With Confidence

Once the vision is clear, the waiting begins. And waiting is where many people grow weary. Biblical waiting is not passive. It is active trust. Isaiah reminds us that those who wait on the Lord renew their strength. Waiting means serving, preparing, and remaining faithful while trusting God with the outcome.

God is not a microwave God. He is a master chef. Microwaves rush the process and damage what they heat. Ovens take time, but they develop depth. Cake cannot be rushed. It requires preparation— ingredients measured, pans prepared, ovens preheated. And while the cake is baking, something happens that you cannot immediately see, but you can sense. The aroma fills the room. Anticipation builds.

You do not open the oven repeatedly, because doing so would ruin the process. Instead, you wait—sometimes peeking through the glass—trusting that what is developing inside will be worth the wait.

That is what confidence looks like.

You prepare even before the cake comes out. You set out the ice cream. You get ready because you believe it is coming. Confidence is not in the cake—it is in the one who put it in the oven.

Conviction Through the Invisible Season

Clarity helps you see. Confidence helps you wait. But conviction keeps you moving when nothing appears to be happening. There were seasons when it looked like nothing was happening with the building process. Meetings were taking place behind the scenes. Conversations were unfolding quietly. Progress was happening invisibly. Conviction kept the work moving even when evidence was scarce.

Discouragement is the enemy's most effective weapon because it steals courage. That is why God repeatedly told Joshua to be strong and courageous. God knew the assignment would be heavy and that discouragement would attempt to stop the journey before fulfillment arrived.

This is why the illustration of pregnancy resonates so deeply. Growth happens long before delivery. The closer the dream gets, the more uncomfortable it may become. Rest becomes difficult. Pressure increases. Everything shifts. But discomfort is not failure— it is formation. Labor is painful, but it produces life.

And when the dream finally arrives, when the vision speaks, when the promise manifests, you realize the delay was never denial. It was development.

Holding On Until It Speaks

Habakkuk's promise still stands.

"The vision will speak."

Not you speaking for it.

Not you forcing it.

Not you defending it endlessly.

It will speak.

It will not lie.

It will surely come.

That language is steady, not emotional. Certain, not speculative. God does not describe the vision as "possible." He describes it as inevitable.

The question is not whether it will speak.

The question is whether you will still be standing when it does.

Because the greatest threat to vision is not opposition — it is abandonment.

Most dreams are not destroyed.

They are released too soon.

People let go when they don't see movement.

They detach when progress slows.

They disengage when applause fades.

But Habakkuk gives us posture.

"If it tarries, wait for it."

Waiting is not passive. Waiting is protective.

Waiting is stewardship.

Your responsibility is not to rush it.

It is to remain faithful to it.

Write it.

Because writing anchors clarity.

Protect it.

Because exposure can damage what is still developing.

Serve while you wait.

Because obedience now prepares you for authority later.

Prepare while it develops.

Because when opportunity arrives, preparation determines whether you are ready or reactive.

Stand with conviction when discouragement tries to steal your courage.

Discouragement will come.

It will whisper that you misheard God.

It will suggest that you miscalculated.

It will highlight what hasn't happened instead of what has.

But conviction remembers what was spoken.

There is a difference between excitement and conviction.

Excitement rises and falls with circumstances.

Conviction stands when circumstances shift.

Joseph had conviction in the pit.

David had conviction in the wilderness.

Noah had conviction while building an ark in dry land.

Conviction is what keeps you building when nobody believes you.

Because vision does not speak on your timetable.

It speaks when it is ready.

And when it speaks, it will confirm that every silent season was preparation.

The vision may be quiet, but it is not dead.

It may be unseen, but it is not inactive.

It may be delayed, but it is not denied.

There is something powerful about allowing a vision to mature.

Fruit picked too early is sour.

Fruit left to ripen is sweet.

God is not teasing you with promise.

He is ripening you for fulfillment.

And here is the anchor that steadies every waiting heart:

What God began, He will finish.

He is not casual with calling.

He is not careless with purpose.

He is not experimental with destiny.

If He authored it, He will conclude it.

The delay is not a sign of rejection.

It is a sign of incompletion.

It is not over.

It is not finished yet.

And sometimes the most spiritual thing you can do is this:

Hold on.

Hold on to the word.

Hold on to the vision.

Hold on to the promise.

Hold on to the God who gave it.

Because when it speaks — and it will — it will not whisper.

It will confirm.

And you will look back at the waiting not with regret, but with gratitude.

Delay is not denial.

It is simply not finished yet.

Reflection

Waiting often reveals more about us than the dream itself. Think about a season in your life when you felt delayed—ready to move forward but unable to control the timing. Like standing at an airport gate watching the screen change, what emotions surfaced during that time? Write honestly about what waiting stirred in you.

Return to the dream God placed in your heart. Write it again—not as a goal, but as a promise. As you write, notice how your understanding has matured. Has the delay refined your vision, or has it tempted you to lower your expectations? Ask God to help you see this season clearly.

Reflect on how you have been waiting. Have you continued preparing like a cake in the oven, trusting the process, or have you grown restless and discouraged? Write about what God may be developing in you while the dream remains out of sight.

Finally, consider conviction. Where has discouragement tried to take your courage? Write one truth that anchors you when progress feels invisible. Let it become a reminder that what feels delayed may actually be forming.

Declaration

I declare that delay is not denial.

I trust God's timing even when I do not understand it.

I will not rush what God is still developing.

I choose to wait with faith, clarity, and confidence.

Even when I cannot see progress, I believe God is working.

I will not allow discouragement to steal my courage.

What God promised will arrive at its appointed time.

I trust the Dream Giver more than the timeline.

Prayer

God, You see me in the waiting. You know how difficult it can be to trust You when progress feels slow and answers seem distant. Yet today, I choose to believe that You are still at work. Help me to hold the vision with clarity and patience. When I am tempted to rush the process, remind me that You are developing something deeper than I can see. Teach me how to wait actively—serving, preparing, and trusting while You work behind the scenes. Strengthen my confidence in You. When discouragement tries to drain my courage, renew my conviction and remind me of what You have spoken. I place my dream back in Your hands and rest in Your faithfulness, trusting that it will speak and arrive right on time. In Jesus' name, Amen.

The Power of A Divine Detour

From Delay to Detour: When God Changes the Route

By now, we have learned that delay is not denial. Chapter 4 reminded us that God's timing, though often uncomfortable, is intentional—and that waiting does not mean God has forgotten what He promised. But there is another reality that often follows delay, one that feels even more disruptive. Sometimes God doesn't just slow you down. Sometimes He sends you another way.

This is where faith is stretched beyond patience and into trust.

A delay allows you to remain on the same road while time expands. A detour, however, changes the road entirely. You are still moving, still believing, still obeying—but the scenery is unfamiliar, the pace feels inefficient, and progress no longer looks like progress. Detours challenge not only how long you are willing to wait, but how deeply you are willing to follow.

The Upper Room Detour: Positioned Before Empowered

Scripture introduces us to this tension immediately after the resurrection.

In Acts 1, Jesus gathers His disciples—men who have already endured fear, grief, and disappointment. They watched Him die. They witnessed Him rise. They are ready to move forward, expecting momentum, direction, and action. But instead of sending them out, Jesus gives them instructions that feel strangely indirect.

"Do not depart from Jerusalem," He tells them, "but wait for the promise of the Father… For John truly baptized with water, but you shall be baptized with the Holy Spirit not many days from now" (Acts 1:4–5).

In other words, don't go where you think you should go yet.

Stay here.

Wait.

Jerusalem was not their destination — it was a detour.

The upper room was not their dream — it was preparation.

Jesus deliberately rerouted them, not because they lacked faith, but because they lacked power. He knew that moving too soon — even with good intentions — would leave them unprepared for what was ahead. They didn't need more information. They needed transformation.

Acts 2 tells us what happened because they obeyed.

"When the day of Pentecost had fully come, they were all with one accord in one place. And suddenly there came a sound from heaven, as of a rushing mighty wind… Then there appeared to them divided tongues, as of fire, and one sat upon each of them. And they were all filled with the Holy Spirit" (Acts 2:1–4).

The *suddenly* did not happen on the main road.

It did not happen while they were advancing.

It happened while they were waiting — together, positioned, and aligned.

Pentecost did not occur because they were ambitious. It happened because they were obedient. God rerouted them so He could position them. He positioned them so He could refine them. He refined them so He could refuel them.

That is the power of a divine detour.

Exit 19: When Experience Meets Obedience

I learned this lesson in one of the most ordinary—and revealing—ways possible: driving to New York.

New York isn't just a destination for me—it's home.

It's muscle memory.

It's history.

It's instinct.

I know the route. I know the traffic patterns. I know where it slows down, where it opens up, where to shift lanes early so you don't get stuck. I've made that drive enough times that my hands almost steer on their own.

Experience creates confidence.

Sometimes too much confidence.

So I got in the car that day, headed up 495, fully assured that I knew exactly where I was going. There was no anxiety. No uncertainty. Just routine.

For reasons I still can't fully explain, I decided to put the address into the GPS.

Maybe it was habit. Maybe it was boredom. Maybe it was discipline.

Waze told me to take Route 50.

I don't take 50 to New York.

That's not my route.

That's not the way I go.

So I shut Waze down and went into Maps. Because Waze gets confused sometimes. I love her—I even call her "Wazy." We have conversations. But if she sounds uncertain, I verify.

Maps told me the same thing.

Take 50.

Now I had an attitude.

Because there are moments when you know what you know—and then there are moments when two trusted authorities agree on something different than your instinct.

I kept driving.

Left lane.

The lane of experience.

The lane of familiarity.

The lane of commitment.

The left lane says, "I've done this before."

The left lane says, "Stick with what you know."

The left lane says, "You don't need new instructions."

And then I reached Exit 19.

That's the decision point.

The right lane begins to open up. Cars are merging. Signals are flashing. There's movement happening that requires intentional shift.

And I felt it.

Not loud.

Not dramatic.

Just a quiet nudge.

Move to the right.

Now this wasn't panic. There was no visible accident ahead. No obvious traffic warning. Just a gentle prompting that disrupted my confidence.

Experience said, "Stay where you are."

The nudge said, "Shift."

Obedience often requires lane changes.

And here's the tension: experience isn't wrong. It just isn't complete.

Experience is built on what has worked.

Obedience is built on what God knows.

At the last possible moment, I moved to the right.

I took Exit 19.

It felt almost foolish. Like abandoning logic. Like questioning my own history. Like surrendering to something I couldn't yet explain.

And because I still had pride working in me, I shut both apps down, pulled them back up, almost daring them to change their minds.

I told myself, "If they reroute me back to 95, I'll swing around and go my way."

But they didn't change.

Both insisted:

Take 50.

And that's when I realized something that applies far beyond highways:

Obedience is not about understanding first.

It's about trusting first.

So I started my detour.

Not because I was convinced.

But because I was prompted.

And here is the deeper spiritual principle:

There are seasons when your history will argue with your hearing.

When what has worked before will compete with what God is saying now.

When experience meets obedience, one of them has to yield.

Experience says, "I've handled this before."

Obedience says, "But this time is different."

Experience says, "Stay in your lane."

Obedience says, "Shift."

And if you are not careful, familiarity will keep you from fresh direction.

The most dangerous thing about experience is not that it is wrong — it is that it feels sufficient.

But God does not only guide beginners.

He guides veterans.

He does not only redirect the inexperienced.

He redirects the confident.

Exit 19 was not just a turn.

It was a test.

Would I trust what I know — or would I trust the nudge?

And here is what I am learning:

Detours often begin at decision points.

And decision points are rarely dramatic.

They are subtle.

They require humility.

They require surrender.

They require you to admit that what you know may not be what you need right now.

So I took the detour.

And what I did not know in that moment was that obedience was protecting me from something I couldn't yet see.

Rerouted by Design: When God Knows What You Don't

I'll be honest—I don't like detours.

I don't like unnecessary delays.

I don't like traffic.

I don't like brake lights stretching for miles in front of me.

And I especially don't like drivers who act like they just learned how to drive—unless they have that little sticker on the back that says "Student Driver," so I can prepare my spirit accordingly.

I'm still in process.

Keep praying for me.

But life has a way of sending us on detours whether we like them or not.

Nobody wakes up asking for the scenic route to disruption.

Nobody plans for the unexpected diagnosis.

The unplanned career shift.

The relationship that didn't last.

The responsibility that arrived without warning.

Yet detours are not rare.

They are regular.

A detour, by definition, is a longer, less direct route taken to avoid something or to reach a destination another way.

Longer.

Less direct.

Another way.

And many of us are living proof of that definition.

We are in careers we didn't originally plan.

We are living in cities we never imagined.

We are carrying responsibilities we didn't anticipate.

Some of us arrived where we are because of decisions we would not make again. Some of us took wrong exits. Some of us ignored signs. Some of us stayed too long. Some of us moved too quickly.

And here is where honesty matters:

Not every detour is divine.

Some are self-inflicted.

But here is where grace enters the story.

Even when the detour is the result of your decision, God is not surprised by it.

He knew about your detour before you ever made the decision.

God's omniscience means He knew your missteps before you misstepped.

He knew the relationship would fail.

He knew the job would end.

He knew the investment would fall through.

He knew the conversation would go wrong.

And yet—He did not abandon you to it.

This is where sovereignty comforts us.

Sovereignty does not mean God caused every turn.

It means nothing catches Him off guard.

There has never been a moment in your life where God said, "I didn't see that coming."

He saw it.

He factored it in.

He built contingencies into your calling.

And what I love about God is that He has a way of turning mess-ups into miracles.

Not by erasing the mistake.

But by redeeming the moment.

Joseph's brothers meant harm.

God meant positioning.

David ran from Saul, hiding in caves he never planned to visit.

But those caves developed a king's character.

Moses fled Egypt after killing a man—a detour born out of impulse.

Yet that desert prepared him to lead millions.

God does not waste roads.

Even the wrong ones.

There are people who look back at their lives with regret and say, "If I hadn't made that choice, I wouldn't be here."

But sometimes "here" is exactly where you needed to be.

You learned humility there.

You learned discipline there.

You learned boundaries there.

You learned dependence there.

You met someone there.

You discovered strength there.

The detour taught you what the direct route could not.

And here is the quiet truth about detours:

They slow you down long enough to see what speed would have hidden.

When you are moving fast, you don't examine much.

You just execute.

But detours force reflection.

They disrupt autopilot.

They make you ask questions.

And sometimes the "longer route" protects you from what the "faster route" would have exposed you to.

That day on Route 50, I didn't know what was ahead.

I only knew what I preferred.

But God knew what I didn't.

He knew about the accident on 95.

He knew about the backup.

He knew about the delay that would have cost me hours.

He knew the meeting I needed to make.

He knew the person I was about to encounter.

Rerouted by design.

That phrase reframes frustration.

Because what feels inefficient to you may be intentional to God.

We call it detour.

God calls it direction.

We call it delay.

God calls it development.

We call it mistake.

God calls it material.

Material for growth.

Material for maturity.

Material for testimony.

If God can take betrayal and build leadership…

If He can take wilderness and build worship…

If He can take a cross and produce resurrection…

Then He can take your detour and turn it into destiny.

You may not like the route.

But if God is guiding it, it is not random.

You are not lost.

You are being led.

And sometimes being rerouted is the clearest evidence that God is still driving.

Positioned in the Pause: The Purpose of Waiting

The disciples didn't choose the upper room. Jesus chose it for them. They had witnessed the resurrection. They had heard the promise of power. In their minds, momentum should have followed miracle. The next logical step was movement.

But instead of sending them out, Jesus sent them up.

Up into a room.

Up into obscurity.

Up into stillness.

They were rerouted by design — and then they were told to wait.

Now that's the hard part.

I don't like waiting. I'll take a detour over sitting still any day. I'll drive ten miles out of my way just to keep moving. Movement feels productive, even if it's inefficient. Waiting feels like stagnation.

But God sometimes positions us in a pause.

And the pause is not punishment. It is preparation.

Waiting seasons often feel wasted — until you realize they are womb seasons. Nothing looks productive in a womb. There are no announcements. No applause. No visible proof of growth. But inside that hidden space, formation is happening. Cells are multiplying. Structure is developing. Strength is building.

And if you rush the womb, you ruin the life.

Premature birth creates fragility. Timing protects formation.

That's what the upper room was — a womb. The disciples thought they were waiting on power, but power was being formed in them while they waited. Unity was deepening. Prayer was strengthening. Ego was dissolving. Dependency was maturing.

Sometimes the promise cannot come because the people are not ready to carry it.

Waiting exposes what rushing hides. When you are forced to sit still, you begin to notice things — your impatience, your anxiety, your desire to control the outcome. Waiting reveals how much of your confidence rests in activity rather than trust.

But waiting also builds endurance.

In the upper room, there was no spotlight. No platform. No applause. Just prayer. And sometimes God will remove visibility so He can increase capacity. If He gives you influence before intimacy, you will perform instead of pray. If He gives you power before patience, you may misuse what He meant to multiply.

Waiting is not inactivity. It is internal activity.

God is aligning motives.

He is strengthening faith.

He is refining character.

He is deepening dependence.

And here is the principle that reframes everything: your location in the waiting determines your elevation in the fulfilling.

They were told where to wait — Jerusalem. Not Galilee. Not Samaria. Jerusalem. The place of crucifixion. The place of confusion. The place of unresolved emotion.

Sometimes God tells you to wait in the very place that tested you.

Because elevation does not come from escape. It comes from obedience.

The Spirit fell in the place of instruction — not preference. And when the appointed time arrived, what had been forming quietly erupted in power. The pause was not empty. It was intentional.

So if you find yourself in a season where movement feels slow and progress feels hidden, do not mistake the womb for a tomb. You are not buried. You are being formed. Nothing may look productive on the outside, but development is happening beneath the surface.

And when it is time — when the moment is full — what was cultivated in private will manifest in power.

Because God never wastes a pause.

Refined on Route 50: What Detours Remove

As I drove Route 50, something shifted.

The scenery changed. The pace changed. The tension changed.

There were no concrete walls pressing in. No aggressive lane merging. No brake lights blinking like warning signals. Instead, there were farms stretching into the distance. Trees lining the horizon. Open sky that felt wide and unhurried.

It was quiet.

And that quiet did something to me.

On 95, you drive defensively. You brace. You anticipate impact. Your mind stays alert for disruption. But on Route 50, the environment itself slowed my spirit down.

I noticed I wasn't gripping the steering wheel as tightly.

I wasn't scanning for sudden stops.

I wasn't calculating lane changes every few seconds.

I was calmer.

I was listening to the music instead of fighting traffic.

I found myself thinking — not about the drive — but about the assignment waiting for me.

That's when I realized something profound:

Detours refine you.

They do not just redirect you — they reshape you.

They remove impatience.

They soften attitudes.

They strip ego.

When you are forced off the path of speed, you discover how addicted you were to urgency. When you are separated from constant friction, you discover how accustomed you had become to tension.

Detours reveal what pressure had been hiding.

There are some things you cannot carry into your next season.

Not because they are sinful — but because they are heavy.

Impatience cannot steward long-term vision.

Ego cannot manage lasting influence.

Restlessness cannot handle sustained growth.

So God takes you on a route that gently removes what would sabotage your future.

Not violently. Not abruptly.

But quietly.

Route 50 did not argue with me. It didn't preach at me. It simply provided space.

And space exposes you to yourself.

That upper room did the same thing.

God refined them before He empowered them.

He disciplined them before He deployed them.

He unified them before He used them.

Acts 1 is uncomfortable because it is unglamorous. No miracles. No crowds. No public demonstrations of power. Just obedience. Just prayer. Just waiting.

But Acts 1 made Acts 2 possible.

We love Acts 2.

We shout over the fire.

We celebrate the sound of a rushing wind.

We highlight three thousand souls added in a day.

But we often forget that the fire fell on people who had first been formed.

God always prepares us for the suddenly.

Suddenly is not spontaneous.

It is scheduled.

It is the collision of preparation and appointed time.

And the suddenly only happens when you are in the right place, with the right posture, and the right people.

The wrong people can keep you from your suddenly.

There came a time in my life when I realized something difficult but necessary: I do not have the time — or the emotional bandwidth — to drag negative people into a future they do not even want.

Some people do not resist your dream because it is impossible. They resist it because it makes them uncomfortable.

They prefer familiarity over faith.

They prefer comfort over calling.

And if you are not careful, you will exhaust yourself trying to convince people to go somewhere they have already decided they do not want to be.

So I made peace with this:

If you don't want to get on board, God bless you. Stay where you are. I'll send you a text from where I'm going.

Because the detour isn't just changing your route — it's changing your circle.

It is separating noise from nurture.

It is distinguishing companions from contributors.

It is refining your environment so your elevation is sustainable.

Not everyone who started with you is meant to arrive with you.

And that realization is not arrogance.

It is alignment.

When God reroutes you, He is not only adjusting geography — He is adjusting relationships, rhythms, and reflexes.

Route 50 was not just about avoiding traffic.

It was about adjusting me.

And then came the final revelation.

Refueled for the Assignment: Protection You Didn't See Coming

Later that day, I turned on the news and discovered there had been a major accident on 95. A four-hour backup. The very route I resisted would have kept me from my assignment. The detour didn't delay me—it protected me.

And when I arrived, something else happened.

After the teaching, a quiet young man approached me. Not flashy. Not loud. He handed me his card and said the teaching changed his life. He owned a finance company. Had an office in Manhattan. Could do deals no bank could touch.

That detour put me in the right place at the right time with the right person.

God was setting me up.

The Accident on 95: Protected by What Frustrated You

Later that day, after I arrived and completed the assignment, I turned on the news.

And there it was.

A major accident on 95.

Not a minor delay. Not a brief slowdown. A shutdown. Multiple lanes blocked. Emergency vehicles lining the shoulder. Cars backed up for miles. Traffic frozen for hours.

Four hours.

The exact stretch I would have been driving.

The exact window of time I would have been in.

The exact direction I insisted I knew.

If I had stayed in the left lane…

If I had ignored the nudge…

If I had trusted familiarity over instruction…

I would have been sitting still.

Frustrated.

Irritated.

Late.

Possibly missing the assignment altogether.

And here's the sobering truth: I wouldn't have known why.

I would have blamed traffic.

I would have blamed timing.

I would have called it "one of those days."

But heaven would have called it protection.

That's when the detour stopped being annoying and started being sacred.

Because what felt inefficient was intentional.

What felt inconvenient was protective.

What felt like delay was deliverance.

Sometimes God doesn't explain the reroute because explanation wouldn't produce obedience. He simply nudges. And only later do you discover what He shielded you from.

How many accidents did you avoid because you were late?

How many rooms did you miss because the door closed?

How many conversations never happened because you were delayed?

There are tragedies you will never know you were spared from.

There are collisions you will never see because God prevented them before you arrived.

And the dangerous part is this: if I had insisted on my route, I would have overruled protection and then blamed the problem.

Obedience doesn't always feel dramatic.

Sometimes it feels like merging right.

But that merge may be the difference between frustration and fulfillment.

Between stagnation and strategy.

Between interruption and impact.

The Right Person at the Right Time: Positioned by Obedience

But protection wasn't the only revelation.

Because after the teaching concluded and people began to disperse, a quiet young man approached me.

He wasn't loud.

He wasn't flashy.

He wasn't trying to impress anyone.

He simply waited.

When the room settled, he stepped forward, shook my hand, and told me the message had shifted something in him. He said it clarified direction. Strengthened resolve. Confirmed timing.

Then, almost casually, he handed me his card.

He owned a finance company.

An office in Manhattan.

Access to capital.

Connections that could structure deals most banks wouldn't even consider.

And in that moment, something clicked.

If I had been stuck on 95…

If I had arrived irritated…

If I had rushed in distracted…

If I had missed the schedule…

That encounter might not have happened.

Or worse — it might have happened, and I wouldn't have recognized it.

That's what detours really do.

They don't just protect you from what you can't see.

They prepare you to recognize what you need to see.

Because divine alignment requires the right time, the right place, and the right posture.

Had I insisted on my route, I might have arrived depleted. And when you're depleted, you miss appointments. You exchange business cards without discernment. You shake hands without sensing significance.

But obedience sharpens awareness.

And when you are positioned properly, you are spiritually alert enough to realize:

This isn't random.

This isn't coincidence.

This isn't casual.

This is coordination.

We often pray for breakthrough without realizing breakthrough sometimes looks like a person.

A connection.

A conversation.

A collaboration.

And the humbling truth is this: the detour I almost resisted became the doorway I couldn't have planned.

Because God sees farther than GPS.

He sees the accident ahead.

He sees the appointment ahead.

He sees the delay.

He sees the alignment.

We call it inconvenience.

He calls it orchestration.

When God reroutes you, it is rarely about one thing.

It is protection and positioning in the same movement.

You are being kept from what would slow you down and carried toward what will move you forward.

The detour didn't cancel the dream.

It conditioned it.

And sometimes the only reason you made it to the right room, at the right time, with the right person…

is because you took Exit 19.

The Revelation: Mercy - Not A Mistake

And that's when I finally understood what divine detours really are. They are not interruptions; they are invitations. Invitations to trust deeper, to listen closer, to surrender tighter. What I thought was a delay was actually direction. What I thought was inconvenience was intelligence. God was not slowing me down — He was aligning me. Protecting me from what I could not see and positioning me for what I could not yet imagine. And maybe that's the real lesson of Route 50: obedience often feels inefficient in the moment, but it proves essential in the end. The detour didn't cancel the dream—it conditioned me for the dream. It refined my instincts, sharpened my awareness, and reminded me that sovereignty is not loud — it whispers. Sometimes the greatest evidence of God's hand on your life is not the doors that open, but the roads He quietly closes. And if you learn to trust Him when He reroutes you, you'll discover that every Exit 19 is not a mistake — it's mercy.

Reflection

Take a moment to pause. Think about the last detour you experienced—something that altered your timeline or redirected your plans. What emotions surfaced during that season? Write honestly about what it felt like to lose control of the route.

Where might God be refining you right now—your patience, discipline, trust, or relationships? Write about what God may be removing so you can carry what's next.

Finally, ask yourself this: *What assignment might God be protecting me for through this detour?*

Declaration

I declare that my detour is not a mistake.

I am rerouted by divine design.

God is refining me, not rejecting me.

My delay is producing discipline and power.

The detour does not cancel my dream—it conditions me for it.

What God promised will come to pass.

I trust God's direction more than my own plan.

Prayer

God, Thank You for directing my steps, even when the route surprises me. Forgive me for resisting Your redirection when I was attached to my own plan. Shape me in the waiting. Refine me in the process. Position me with the right people, in the right posture, at the right time. I trust that every detour is purposeful and every pause is preparing me for what You promised. In Jesus' name, Amen.

The Test That Resurrects The Dream

Scripture Focus: Genesis 22:1–14
A Bridge from Delay and Detour into Testing

If Chapter 4 taught us how to wait without quitting—and Chapter 5 taught us how to follow God even when the route changes—then Chapter 6 takes us into a moment that feels more intense than delay or detour. Because sometimes the dream isn't just postponed. Sometimes the dream is tested.

This is the part of the journey most people don't announce. We celebrate blessings, but we whisper about surrender. We post the promotion, but we keep quiet about the pressure. We like the promise, but we struggle when the promise is challenged. Yet if we are going to talk honestly about resurrecting your dream, we have to tell the truth: the dream may be God-given, but it will still be God-tested.

There comes a moment in every dreamer's life when you look back and realize, *That was it. That was the test.* The season that forced you to decide what mattered most. The moment that demanded more than inspiration—it demanded obedience. The circumstance that asked, not do you believe, but do you trust Me with what I gave you?

And if you haven't reached that moment yet, keep living. It's coming.

Because life has a way of "lifing." Dreams get buried under responsibility. Purpose gets postponed under pressure. And even when God resurrects what you buried—bringing it back to the surface—there often comes a test that touches the deepest question in your soul: Do you love the dream more than you love the Dream Giver?

That's where Genesis 22 meets us.

The Long Road to the Promise

Abraham is not just a father in the natural; he is a father in the spiritual. He is Isaac's father, yes—but he is also the father of many nations, the father of faith, the man whose name becomes permanently connected to believing God when life doesn't make sense. But before Abraham became a hero in Scripture, he was an old man with no children and a promise that seemed unreasonable.

God spoke to Abraham when he was about seventy-five and told him, in essence, *I'm going to make you the father of many nations.* It sounds powerful until you remember the details. Abraham was old. Sarah was old. Their biology didn't cooperate with the prophecy. And that tension—between what God says and what you see—is the tension most of us live with.

Then time passed. Not weeks. Not months. Years. Decades. Almost twenty-five years of waiting, believing, trying to remain hopeful while the calendar kept turning. And then, finally, God did exactly what He said. Isaac arrived. The dream showed up. The promise became personal. Abraham wasn't just holding a prophecy anymore; he was holding a boy.

And you would think that once the dream is in your arms, the hardest part is over.

But sometimes the hardest test doesn't come before the dream.

Sometimes it comes after you receive it.

When God Tests What You Love

Genesis 22 opens with a sentence that should stop every dreamer in their tracks: "Now it came to pass after these things that God tested Abraham…" The Bible doesn't soften it. It doesn't hide it. It simply names it. A test is coming.

God calls Abraham by name: "Abraham." And Abraham responds the way a person responds who has learned to recognize the voice of God: "Here I am."

Then God says something that can take your breath away if you really hear it: "Take now your son, your only son, Isaac, whom you love… and offer him."

God doesn't just say "your son." He says "your only son." And then, as if to underline the tenderness of the request, He adds, "whom you love." God is touching the most sensitive place in Abraham's life— the place where love lives, the place where hope finally took root.

And then God does what He often does with Abraham: He tells him to go without giving him the full directions up front. "Go to the land of Moriah… on one of the mountains of which I shall tell you." That means Abraham must start moving without knowing every detail.

God and Abraham have this kind of relationship—God often says go and then tells him where he's going after he leaves. It's a strange thing for our modern minds because we like clarity before we move. But faith rarely works like that. Faith moves with what God has said, even when the map is incomplete.

Obedience Without the Full Map

And Abraham rose early the next morning.

That detail matters because it shows us something about his obedience. He didn't procrastinate. He didn't negotiate. He didn't say, "Lord, let me think about it." He got up, saddled the donkey, gathered the wood, and started walking toward the assignment.

Sometimes you can tell what you really believe by what you do early.

Abraham travels three days. Three days is a long time to walk with a heavy instruction. Three days gives fear plenty of time to argue. Three days gives doubt room to preach. Three days gives your emotions an opportunity to take over. Yet Abraham keeps moving.

Then he looks up and sees the place afar off.

And right there, in that moment, Abraham speaks something that reveals the inner engine of his faith. He turns to the young men traveling with him and says: "Stay here with the donkey; the lad and I will go yonder and worship, and we will come back to you."

We will come back.

Not I will come back. Not I'll see what happens. Abraham says, we will come back.

That statement doesn't match the visible assignment. God told him to offer Isaac. Abraham says, "We're coming back." Something is happening inside Abraham that is deeper than logic. And Hebrews 11 explains it: Abraham concluded that God was able to raise Isaac from the dead. In other words, Abraham's faith wasn't only in the promise. His faith was in the God who could keep the promise even if the process looked like it was contradicting it.

This is what mature faith looks like: believing God so strongly that you obey Him even when the instruction seems to threaten the outcome.

The Question That Every Dream Must Answer

Abraham places the wood on Isaac's back and carries the fire and the knife. The two of them walk together. And then Isaac asks a question that makes the whole story painfully human: "My father… we have the fire and the wood, but where is the lamb?"

Isaac is not a baby in this story. He's likely a teenager by now — strong enough to carry wood, old enough to understand sacrifice, aware enough to notice what's missing. And that's what makes the next moment even more weighty. Isaac knows something is different. Abraham knows everything is different. Yet they keep walking.

Abraham answers with a line that still preaches: "My son, God will provide for Himself the lamb."

Sometimes you have to speak provision before you see it. Sometimes you have to declare what God will do while you are still walking toward what you don't understand.

The Altar: Where Dreams Are Purified, Not Punished

They arrive at the place God indicated. Abraham builds an altar. He places the wood in order. Then he binds Isaac and lays him on the altar.

And it's right here that the story confronts us with the depth of trust.

Isaac could have run. Isaac could have fought. Isaac could have resisted. Yet he allows his aging father to tie him down. That is a whole series by itself, but it points to something important: Abraham must have raised Isaac in such a way that Isaac trusted the God in his father.

That becomes a word for every father, every leader, every parent, every person with influence: raise those connected to you in such a way that even when they don't fully understand the situation, they can still trust the God working through you. There will be seasons when your family's faith isn't fully formed—but they can lean on your faith while theirs is being built.

Then Abraham stretches out his hand, takes the knife, and prepares to slay his son.

This is the test.

Not the promise. Not the prophecy. The test is what happens when God touches what you love. The test is what happens when God requires you to release what you prayed for. The test is what happens when you realize the dream is a gift—yes—but it is not yours to worship.

And this is where our humanity wrestles, because we all say, "God, give me…" but we don't always say, "God, You can have…" Yet if God blessed you with it, then it belongs to Him—your child, your career, your finances, your opportunities, your gifts, your dreams.

That truth is why people struggle with giving. It's not the amount— it's the acknowledgment of ownership. If I struggle to trust God with a portion, what happens when He presses on something bigger? The issue is rarely money. The issue is trust.

And this is a line we all must face: what you are willing to release reveals who you really trust.

The Deliverance That Happens in the Decision

Abraham releases Isaac internally before he ever releases him physically. He makes the decision in his heart before he sees the ram. And there's a principle here that can free you: sometimes deliverance is in the decision. Sometimes the breakthrough doesn't come when the situation changes; it comes when you decide, "God, I trust You even here."

But we should also tell the truth about surrender: surrender is not a magic trick. Abraham got a ram, but your story may not look exactly like Abraham's story. Sometimes God replaces. Sometimes God removes. Sometimes God redirects. The point isn't that God always gives you an alternative. The point is that God always proves Himself faithful, even when the outcome looks different than you expected.

Jehovah Jireh: Provision Revealed in the Right Place

Abraham raises the knife—then heaven interrupts.

"Abraham, Abraham!"

He responds again: "Here I am."

"Do not lay your hand on the lad… for now I know that you fear God, since you have not withheld your son, your only son, from Me."

Then Abraham lifts his eyes and sees what God had already arranged: a ram caught in a thicket by its horns. The provision was there, but it was revealed at the right moment, in the right place, after the right posture of obedience.

Abraham offers the ram instead of his son and names the place: Jehovah Jireh—The Lord Will Provide.

Not "The Lord Did Provide."

Not "The Lord Used To Provide."

But "The Lord Will Provide."

Because Abraham understands something every dreamer must learn: provision is not only a testimony from yesterday—it's a promise for tomorrow.

There are places in your life you need to rename. Seasons you survived. Doors God opened. Moments God sustained you. You need to call some spaces "Jehovah Jireh" because God provided when you didn't know how it would work out.

The Dream Isn't Destroyed—It's Deepened

And here is the resurrection in the text: the dream is not destroyed by the test—the dream is deepened by it.

Isaac is received.

Isaac is released.

And the promise is resurrected—not because the dream was replaced, but because Abraham's faith was expanded.

Hebrews makes it plain: Abraham believed God could raise Isaac from the dead. That means Abraham's confidence was not in the method; it was in the Maker. Not in the process; in the Promise Keeper. Not in the timeline; in the God who can do what He said by any means necessary.

That's the kind of faith that resurrects dreams.

Because some dreams can only be sustained by surrender. Some promises can only be carried by people who have learned that the altar is not a place of punishment—it's a place of preparation. And some breakthrough only happens when you finally accept this: if God orders it, He can pay for it. But if you order the dream in your flesh, you'll end up paying the bill with your peace.

This chapter isn't just about Abraham. It's about us—about what happens when your dream meets its test. About the moment God asks, "Do you trust Me with what I gave you?" About the freedom that comes when you realize the dream was never meant to replace God—it was meant to flow through your relationship with Him.

So don't run from the test. Don't curse the altar. Don't abandon the place where God reveals Himself as Jehovah Jireh.

The dream is received.

The dream must be released.

And the dream will be resurrected.

Reflection

Sit with Abraham's story as a mirror, not a museum piece. Where have you felt God pressing on something you love? Where has obedience felt costly? Write honestly about what has been hardest for you to surrender.

Return to the dream God gave you. Have you ever held it so tightly that it began to feel like it was holding you? Write about what part of your dream—or your life—might need to go back on the altar, not to be destroyed, but to be purified.

Consider what "release" could mean for you right now. Release does not always mean losing something. Sometimes it means loosening your grip, letting God lead, letting God decide timing, method, and outcome. Write what it would look like to trust God even if the process remains unclear.

Finally, remember provision. Write one "Jehovah Jireh" moment from your past—when God made a way you couldn't predict. Then write what you need God to provide now, not as a demand, but as an act of faith.

Declaration

I declare that I trust God with what He has given me.

I will not worship the dream more than the Dream Giver.

I will not fear the altar, because God meets me there.

When God tests me, He is not trying to break me—He is building me.

I release control and receive God's provision.

Jehovah Jireh is my God—He will provide.

What God promised will live, even through the test.

My dream is being resurrected.

Prayer

God,

Thank You for the dream You placed in me and the promise You spoke over my life. Today I admit that surrender is not always easy.

There are things I love, things I value, and things I fear losing. But I choose to trust You.

Help me release what You require without resentment or panic. Strengthen my faith when the process doesn't make sense. Teach me to keep listening as I walk, so I don't miss Your direction and end up outside Your provision.

When my heart feels heavy, remind me that You are Jehovah Jireh—the God who provides, the God who protects, the God who keeps His word. I place my dream back in Your hands. Resurrect it, refine it, and realign it with Your purpose.

In Jesus' name,

Amen.

Living The Dream

Scripture Focus: Ephesians 3:20–21

There is a moment every dreamer imagines, but few prepare for—the moment when the dream actually begins to live.

For most of us, the dream begins quietly. It appears as a whisper in prayer, a thought that refuses to leave, a vision that lingers long after the moment has passed. We picture the doors opening. We imagine the opportunity arriving. We anticipate the breakthrough.

But what we rarely talk about is what happens after the door opens.

We spend years praying for opportunity, yet very little time preparing for responsibility. We ask God for expansion, but we do not always consider the discipline required to manage what expands. We pray for overflow, but we do not always develop the order necessary to sustain it.

So when the dream finally arrives, it can surprise us.

Not because it is not beautiful.

But because it is heavy.

Fulfillment, it turns out, carries weight.

Answered prayer is not just celebration—it is stewardship.

That is why resurrection is not only about the dream coming back to life. Resurrection is also about learning how to live once the dream returns.

This is where Ephesians 3:20–21 becomes more than a scripture we shout about—it becomes a guide for how we live.

"Now to Him who is able to do exceedingly abundantly above all that we ask or think… according to the power that works in us… to Him be glory…"

Most people quote this passage to celebrate God's ability to exceed our expectations. And that is certainly true. But Paul's emphasis is not only on God's ability—it is on God's purpose.

Because the verse does not end with abundance.

It ends with glory.

"Unto Him be glory…"

That means every blessing carries responsibility. Every opportunity carries expectation. Every answered prayer carries purpose beyond our comfort.

God answers, yes.

God elevates, yes.

God expands, yes.

But every increase is connected to a greater assignment—to reflect His glory.

Overflow is not just about having more. It is about handling more in a way that honors the One who gave it.

That is the part many people overlook when they pray for increase.

Most of us pray for "more" the way children ask for candy. We know what we want, but we have not thought deeply about what it will require.

We pray for money but have not learned management.

We pray for influence but have not developed integrity.

We pray for opportunity but have not cultivated discipline.

We pray for a spouse but have not matured emotionally.

We pray for ministry but have not embraced the weight of responsibility.

And if we are honest, many of us have already lived through this lesson.

God answered.

But we were not ready.

That is why this chapter matters.

Living the dream is about learning how to carry what God gives without losing what God is building in you.

A resurrected dream must be sustained with resurrected discipline.

Because the habits that helped you survive Saturday will not always sustain you in Sunday.

You cannot live at a new level with an old mindset.

Living the dream requires three things:

Seizing the season.

Stewarding the stretch.

Staying strong in the Savior.

The Season That Must Be Seized

When God gives you opportunity, you cannot treat it casually.

Some seasons are windows, not walls.

They open for a moment.

And if you ignore them, they close.

Seizing the season means recognizing that what you prayed for has arrived—and responding with intention.

Many people ask God for financial increase. They pray for better opportunities, expanded resources, and new doors. And sometimes God answers in very practical ways: a raise, a new job, a contract, a business opportunity.

But here is the challenge: some people prayed for more money when what they actually needed was more wisdom.

Because money does not heal poor habits—it reveals them.

Increase does not fix what is broken.

It magnifies what already exists.

Someone who manages poorly with little will often manage poorly with more. The spending patterns remain the same, only the numbers change.

Instead of building stability, the increase simply upgrades the stress.

They celebrate the blessing but ignore the responsibility.

They buy the car but neglect the savings.

They enjoy the reward but avoid the planning.

And when difficulty arrives, it appears as though God failed—when the truth is they never seized the season to develop stewardship.

Seizing the season requires more than gratitude.

It requires intentional growth.

Some blessings are not just gifts.

They are assignments.

The same principle applies to business dreams.

People pray, "Lord, let me own a business."

They imagine freedom, flexibility, independence. They envision the joy of building something meaningful for their family and community.

And then the door opens.

But what follows the dream is responsibility.

Rent must be paid.

Employees must be managed.

Inventory must be maintained.

Customers must be served.

The dream becomes real—and reality demands discipline.

The people who thrive in those moments understand something important: when the door opens, you do not just celebrate.

You study.

You ask questions.

You learn what you do not know.

You build systems.

You surround yourself with people who strengthen your weaknesses.

Because a dream treated like fantasy eventually becomes frustration.

But a dream treated like a responsibility becomes legacy.

I learned this lesson personally when I made the decision to return to competitive softball after more than fifteen years away from the game.

The fundamentals were still there. I understood the sport. I knew the strategy.

But I quickly realized that experience alone was not enough for this season.

New cleats and a new glove would not protect me if I approached the game with old habits.

The body I had now was not the body I had fifteen years ago. And if I ignored that reality, I would pay for it.

Seizing this season required preparation—not nostalgia.

The game had not changed.

But I had.

And sometimes we miss the season not because God failed to open the door—but because we insisted on walking through it unprepared.

New seasons often arrive with discomfort.

But discomfort does not mean disqualification.

Sometimes discomfort simply means development is happening.

The Stretch That Sustains the Dream

Every fulfilled dream requires stretching.

New levels stretch your schedule.

New opportunities stretch your capacity.

New visibility stretches your character.

Stretching is the hidden requirement of growth.

When I returned to softball, one of the first pieces of advice I received had nothing to do with hitting or throwing.

It was simple.

Stretch.

Stretching would help me run faster, throw farther, and compete without injuring myself.

At first it seemed small.

But I quickly realized it was essential.

Stretching did not weaken me—it prepared me.

The more I stretched, the more capable I became.

The same principle applies spiritually.

God stretches us so success will not break us.

He stretches our patience so pressure will not crush us.

He stretches our discipline so opportunity will not overwhelm us.

He stretches our humility so success will not poison our character.

Consider marriage.

People pray passionately for a spouse. They fast, attend conferences, and ask God to bring the right person into their lives.

Then the relationship begins.

The wedding happens.

The vows are spoken.

The dream becomes real.

But that is when stewardship begins.

Because a spouse is not a trophy.

A spouse is a trust.

Love must be nurtured.

Communication must be cultivated.

Patience must be practiced.

Some people lose what they prayed for because they never learned how to honor it once they had it.

And ministry?

Ministry stretches you in ways few people anticipate.

Many people pray, "Lord, use me."

They imagine preaching, influence, and impact.

But ministry is not only about speaking.

It is about carrying.

Carrying people's pain.

Carrying responsibility.

Carrying expectation.

God does not just call you to speak.

He calls you to shepherd.

Stretching is not punishment.

It is preparation.

God enlarges your capacity so you can carry the dream without collapsing under its weight.

Strength That Comes from the Savior

Here is the anchor that keeps the dream from becoming an idol:

Your strength is not in the dream.

Your strength is in the Savior.

Preparation matters.

Discipline matters.

Stretching matters.

But none of them replace dependence on God.

Even after stretching for softball, I still had to respect my limits. Recovery mattered. Rest mattered. Wisdom mattered.

Preparation positioned me.

But wisdom preserved me.

Success has a subtle way of whispering dangerous lies.

It can convince you that you did it alone.

It can persuade you that you no longer need prayer.

It can tempt you to rely on your gifts instead of God.

But living the dream means remembering what brought you here.

Prayer.

Faith.

Dependence on God.

That is why Paul ends Ephesians 3 the way he does.

"To Him be glory."

The dream is not the glory.

God is.

Living the dream means staying rooted.

You never outgrow prayer.

You never outgrow worship.

You never outgrow accountability.

Because if God did it, God must sustain it.

Living the dream means keeping your hands open.

Open to receive.

Open to surrender.

Because when you live this way—seizing the season, stewarding the stretch, and staying strong in the Savior—you do not simply experience success.

You experience purpose.

And that is the real resurrection.

Not just that the dream lives.

But that you live well while it does.

And perhaps that is the greatest surprise of all. Living the dream does not end the journey—it expands it. What once felt like the final destination often becomes the doorway to a new horizon. Because the God who resurrects dreams is not limited to one chapter of your life. The same God who helped you survive Friday, who sustained you through Saturday, and who raised the dream again on Sunday, is also the God who continues to write the story beyond what you first imagined. Sometimes the dream you fought so hard to reclaim becomes the foundation for a dream you never saw coming. And when that moment arrives—when life shifts again, when seasons change again, when God begins stirring something new in your spirit again—you realize that resurrection is not just an event. It is a rhythm. God does not only restore what was lost; He also awakens what is next. And that realization leads us to the next and perhaps most courageous step in the journey: learning how to dream again.

Reflection

Think about a time when you prayed for something and then realized it required more stewardship than you expected. What did you learn about yourself in that season—your habits, your weaknesses, your maturity? Write the story honestly.

Now consider the dream you are pursuing—or the dream God has revived. If it came to pass tomorrow, what areas of your life would need to grow immediately in order to sustain it? Write what you would need in your character, your schedule, your finances, your relationships, and your spiritual life.

Where are you being stretched right now? Is it in patience, responsibility, commitment, discipline, or humility? Describe the stretch. Then write how this stretch might actually be God enlarging your capacity.

Finally, identify one discipline you will commit to in order to stay rooted in the Savior while you pursue success. It may be prayer, fasting, budgeting, counseling, accountability, sabbath rest, or time in Scripture. Write your commitment as a promise to God and to yourself.

Declaration

I declare that I will live what God has given me with wisdom and humility.

I will seize the season and honor the opportunity.

I will steward the stretch and grow with discipline.

I will not mishandle what I prayed for.

I will not treat people like inconveniences when they are answered prayers.

I will not chase success and lose my soul.

My strength is in the Savior, not in success.

God is able—and God will sustain what He has resurrected in me.

I will live the dream for God's glory.

Prayer

God,

Thank You for being the God who answers prayer and resurrects dreams. I don't want to simply receive what I asked for—I want to steward it well.

Give me wisdom for every new season. When You increase me, teach me how to manage increase with maturity. When You bless me with opportunity, give me discipline to honor it. When You bless me with relationships, teach me how to love with patience and humility. When You call me into purpose, prepare me for the challenges that come with it.

Keep me rooted in You. Guard my heart from pride, entitlement, and distraction. Help me remain grateful, accountable, and faithful. Let my life be proof that You are able to do exceedingly abundantly above all I can ask or think—and let it bring You glory.

In Jesus' name,

Amen.

Dare to Dream Again

Scripture Focus: Isaiah 43:18-19

There comes a moment in every life when God does not take something away—but invites you to build on what He has already done.

This is where many people misunderstand seasons. We assume that when God speaks of something *"new,"* it must mean that what came before has failed, faded, or died. But Scripture paints a different picture. God is not dismissive of the past—He is developmental.

He does not waste experiences.

He does not discard obedience.

He does not erase seasons that shaped you.

Instead, He uses them as momentum.

God builds forward.

Isaiah records God saying something that sounds almost shocking at first:

"Do not remember the former things,

Nor consider the things of old.

Behold, I will do a new thing…"

At first glance, it sounds like God is telling His people to forget their history. But that is not what the text is saying. God is not instructing them to erase their memory—He is warning them not to become anchored to it.

There is a difference between **remembering with gratitude** and **remaining stuck in familiarity**.

God honors the past.

But He refuses to be confined by it.

This chapter is not about letting an old dream die.

It is about allowing God to use what was to propel you into what can be.

Because life is not about reaching one dream and stopping.

Life is about being willing to **dream again.**

When God Shifts the Season Without Negating the Story

Seasons shift not because something went wrong—but because growth requires movement.

There are times when God allows a dream to be fulfilled, sustained, and even celebrated—and then gently begins to stir something new within you. Nothing is broken. Nothing is wasted. Nothing has failed.

But something is changing.

And often, the most uncomfortable part of change is not loss—it is uncertainty.

You start to feel it internally before anything changes externally.

What once energized you now feels familiar.

What once challenged you now feels mastered.

What once stretched you now feels predictable.

And instead of recognizing that as growth, many people interpret it as dissatisfaction.

But what if it is not dissatisfaction at all?

What if it is invitation?

God uses seasons to teach lessons, develop discipline, refine character, and reveal purpose. And once those lessons have been learned, God does not trap us in repetition.

He invites us forward.

The danger is not in honoring what God did.

The danger is in refusing to move when God whispers,

"There's more."

Because the same God who gave you yesterday's dream is still creative enough to give you tomorrow's.

Allowing the Old to Become the Fuel for the New

God is a master at repurposing.

He takes experiences, skills, relationships, failures, successes, and even disappointments and uses them as building blocks for what comes next.

Nothing is lost.

Nothing is irrelevant.

Everything becomes resource.

The wisdom you gained in the last season becomes guidance in the next.

The discipline you learned becomes stability.

The faith you exercised becomes confidence.

The pain you endured becomes compassion.

Even mistakes become teachers.

God wastes nothing.

When God does something new, He is not starting from scratch—He is building on what already exists.

And sometimes the greatest preparation for the next dream is hidden in the previous one.

A Mother Who Dared to Dream Again

That truth is deeply personal to me.

My mother was a small woman with a big dream.

Her dream was not flashy or public. She wasn't chasing recognition or applause. Her dream was simple but powerful—she wanted her four boys to grow up, be successful, and have opportunities greater than the ones she had been given.

But life did not unfold easily.

After walking through a difficult divorce, she found herself standing in the middle of a reality that many people know all too well: love alone would not sustain a household.

She needed provision.

She needed stability.

She needed vision.

So she did something that required tremendous courage.

She dared to dream again.

She went back to school when quitting would have been understandable.

She earned her degree when exhaustion could have justified surrender.

She kept pushing when the easier option would have been to settle.

And eventually, she became the **head of nursing at St. Joseph Medical Center in Yonkers, New York.**

That decision changed everything.

Her daring to dream again allowed her four boys the opportunity to live their dreams.

Because she chose resilience over resignation, her sons grew up believing that adversity was not the end of the story.

Her grind became our ground.

Her faith became our framework.

Her obedience became our opportunity.

But here is the honest truth: her dream came with cost.

There were long hours.

There were late nights.

There were seasons when she was out of the home because she was doing what she had to do to provide, protect, and prepare a future for her children.

Her pursuit shaped the way we grew up.

It taught us independence earlier than most.

It taught us responsibility sooner than expected.

It formed a resilience in us that did not come from comfort—but from necessity.

Yet even in her absence, we never felt abandoned.

She made sure of that.

Love was consistent.

Expectations were clear.

Support was constant.

Even when she was tired.

Even when she was stretched.

Even when she was carrying more than anyone should have to carry alone.

She remained present in the ways that mattered most.

Because absence without intention creates wounds.

But sacrifice with love creates strength.

The Generational Power of Dreaming Again

The way she lived, worked, and persevered did more than shape our childhood—it shaped our future.

It influenced the way we now raise our own families.

It shaped our work ethic.

It formed our understanding of responsibility.

Her example taught us something powerful:

Responsibility is love in action.

Presence is more than proximity.

And sometimes doing what is necessary in one season creates stability for generations to come.

She did not just change her own trajectory.

She altered ours.

And that is the often-unseen power of dreaming again.

When you live your dream, it does not stop with you.

It impacts everyone within your **sphere of influence**.

Your willingness to grow gives others permission to believe.

Your courage creates capacity for those watching you.

Your faith becomes the framework through which others learn how to trust God with their own future.

God used her education, her leadership, and her perseverance not simply to elevate her—but to create possibility for her children and perspective for their children.

Her new dream did not replace her original hope for her family.

It fulfilled it in a greater way.

That is how God works.

When God does something new, He is not starting from scratch— He is building generationally.

He is using one person's obedience to unlock another person's destiny.

And that is why dreaming again is never selfish.

It is stewardship.

Because sometimes God allows you to dream again not just for your sake—but for everyone connected to you.

Choosing Hope Over Comfort

One of the greatest temptations in life is not failure.

It is comfort.

Comfort whispers softly:

Stay where you are.

You've already done enough.

You've already proven yourself.

Why risk disappointment again?

Comfort disguises itself as wisdom.

But often it is simply fear wearing a polite voice.

Faith, however, always pulls forward.

Dreaming again means believing God beyond what you have already seen Him do.

It means trusting that the same God who was faithful before is faithful still.

It means accepting that growth often requires reimagining what is possible.

God does not ask you to dream again because He is dissatisfied with you.

He invites you to dream again because **He sees more in you.**

The new thing God is doing does not erase the old thing.

It expands it.

Life Is About Being Willing to Dream Again

Dreaming again is not denial.

It is declaration.

It declares that your best days are not behind you.

It declares that God's creativity has not run dry.

It declares that purpose does not expire with age, experience, or accomplishment.

When you dare to dream again, you are saying:

"God, I trust You not only with my past and my present—but with my future."

And that is where renewal lives.

That is where joy returns.

That is where faith stays alive.

Because resurrection was never meant to be a one-time event.

Resurrection was always meant to become a way of living.

Reflection

Take time to reflect on someone in your life—past or present—who dared to dream again when circumstances made it difficult. What sacrifices did their decision require? How did their courage shape the opportunities, stability, or perspective you now have? Write about how their obedience influenced your life, even in ways you did not recognize at the time.

Now consider your own life. Where has God asked you to keep moving forward even when the cost felt heavy? Are there seasons where pursuing what was necessary meant your time, energy, or availability shifted? Write honestly about the tension between responsibility and presence, and how love can still be communicated even when life demands more.

Reflect on the people within your current sphere of influence—your children, family, congregation, mentees, coworkers, or friends. How might your willingness to dream again create permission for them to believe more boldly in their own future? Write about the legacy you are actively shaping through your decisions today.

Finally, ask yourself this question:

If someone were to look back on this season of my life, what would they learn about faith, perseverance, and trust in God from the way I lived?

Write one intentional step you will take to pursue what God is stirring in you—while remaining grounded in love, integrity, and purpose.

Declaration

I declare that my life is still unfolding.

I honor what God has done, and I trust what God is doing now.

I refuse to live anchored to comfort or confined by familiarity.

I believe God uses every season to prepare me for the next.

I am not finished. God is not finished.

I dare to dream again—with faith, hope, and expectation.

Prayer

God,

Thank You for every season You have carried me through. Thank You for the dreams You fulfilled, the lessons You taught, and the growth You produced in me.

Today, I choose not to cling to the past, but to trust You with the future.

If You are stirring something new in me, give me the courage to follow.

If You are expanding my vision, give me the faith to believe again.

Help me see new possibilities not as threats, but as invitations.

Use everything I've been through as fuel for where You are taking me.

I place my future back in Your hands—with expectation, not fear.

In Jesus' name,

Amen.

The Dreamer's Declaration

Scripture Focus: Philippians 1:6

Every journey needs a moment of resolve. Not a pause.

Not a reflection.

A resolve.

After the waiting.

After the darkness.

After the delay, the detour, the testing, the stretching, and the renewal—there comes a moment when the dreamer must decide who they are going to be now.

Because resurrecting your dream was never just about getting something back.

It was about becoming someone new.

There comes a moment when the conversation with God shifts. No longer are you asking *"Why did this happen?"* Instead, you begin asking *"What am I supposed to do with what You've done in me?"*

That shift changes everything.

Paul captures this moment perfectly when he writes in Philippians 1:6:

"Being confident of this very thing, that He who has begun a good work in you will complete it until the day of Jesus Christ."

This is not a verse about comfort.

It is a verse about completion.

Paul writes it from prison, not prosperity. Chains were on his wrists and uncertainty surrounded his circumstances. Yet even in confinement he spoke with confidence. Why? Because he understood something that every dreamer must eventually learn:

God does not start things casually.

He does not resurrect dreams partially.

He does not revive vision only to abandon it halfway.

What God begins, He finishes.

What God promises, He completes.

What God resurrects, He sustains.

And Chapter 9 is where we stop rehearsing what happened to the dream—and start declaring what will happen because of it.

From Surviving to Standing

There was a time when survival felt like victory.

Getting through the night.

Making it past the pain.

Holding on through the confusion.

But survival is not the goal.

Transformation is.

God never intended for you to spend the rest of your life in recovery mode. He did not bring you through the valley so you could build a house there. He brought you through so you could stand on the other side with perspective, authority, and clarity.

Joseph did not remain in the pit—he ruled in purpose.

The Shunammite woman did not remain in grief—she stood in restoration.

Lazarus did not stay wrapped in grave clothes—he walked out alive.

Abraham did not lose the promise—he discovered the Provider.

And your story does not end where it hurt.

Pain may have been a chapter—but it was never the conclusion.

The reason God resurrects dreams is not simply to prove His power. God resurrects dreams to reposition your posture.

At some point you stop saying:

"I'm just trying to make it."

And you start saying:

"I know who I am."

This chapter marks that shift.

Because surviving builds endurance—but standing builds identity.

Owning the Work God Is Doing in You

A declaration is not a wish.

It is a decision spoken aloud.

It is the moment when your voice catches up with your transformation. It is when what God has been doing internally finally becomes something you are willing to acknowledge externally.

A declaration is the sound of alignment.

It is the moment you stop shrinking your voice to match your past and start aligning your words with your future.

Too many people reach the end of a hard season but never claim the authority that came with it.

They survived—but they never stood.

They endured—but they never owned the transformation.

But this is where the dreamer learns something vital:

God did not just change your circumstances.

He changed you.

Your discernment is sharper.

Your faith is deeper.

Your compassion is richer.

Your obedience is stronger.

The things that once intimidated you now instruct you.

The situations that once overwhelmed you now reveal how far you have grown.

You are not who you were before the dream died.

And you are not who you were when it came back.

That is why the declaration matters.

Because if you never acknowledge what God has done in you, you may accidentally continue living beneath it.

Declarations anchor identity.

They remind you who you are when life tries to convince you otherwise.

The Dreamer's Declaration Is a Line in the Sand

At some point, you stop negotiating with fear.

You stop explaining yourself to people who never carried your weight.

You stop asking permission to walk in what God confirmed.

You stop apologizing for growth.

The Dreamer's Declaration becomes a line in the sand.

A spiritual moment where you quietly but firmly decide:

"I am no longer living from what broke me.

I am living from what built me."

This is where you declare that delay did not disqualify you.

Detours did not derail you.

Testing did not terminate you.

This is where you recognize that God used everything.

Every tear.

Every stretch.

Every sleepless night.

Every sacrifice.

None of it was random.

None of it was wasted.

It was preparation.

And this declaration does not make you arrogant.

It makes you anchored.

Because arrogance says *"Look what I did."*

But a dreamer's declaration says:

"Look what God brought me through."

Living as Proof That Resurrection Is Real

Here is the final truth this book leads to:

Your life is now evidence.

Not because you are perfect.

Not because you never struggled again.

But because you kept trusting God when it would have been easier to quit.

Resurrection is not simply something that happened to Jesus.

Resurrection is something God continues to demonstrate in the lives of His people.

Dreams come back.

Hope returns.

Purpose rises.

And people notice.

People may not read this book—but they will read you.

They will watch how you lead.

How you love.

How you recover.

How you respond when life shifts again.

And when they ask, "How did you make it?"

Your answer will not be complicated.

You will say:

God finished what He started.

That is resurrection living.

The Dreamer's Declaration

This is not something you read quietly.

This is something you own.

This is something you speak.

Declaration

I declare that God is not finished with me.

What He started, He will complete.

My past did not cancel my purpose.

My delays did not diminish my destiny.

My detours did not disqualify me.

I have survived the night, and I am stepping into the day.

I release fear, regret, and hesitation.

I receive faith, courage, and clarity.

I will live as proof that resurrection is real.

I will walk boldly in what God has restored.

I will dream—and I will dare to dream again.

My life will glorify God.

My obedience will outlive me.

And my story is still being written.

Reflection

Look back over your journey through this book. What moment, chapter, or story felt most personal to you? Why do you believe God highlighted that part of the journey?

What has changed in you—not just around you—because of what you've walked through? Write about the internal growth you may not have recognized before.

Now write your own Dreamer's Declaration. Use your own words, but let it reflect confidence, trust, and expectation. This is not about perfection—it's about posture.

Finally, ask yourself: What does it look like for me to live as proof that resurrection is real? Write one way your life can reflect God's restoring power to someone else.

Closing Prayer

God,

Thank You for never abandoning the work You started in me. Thank You for meeting me in the dark, sustaining me through the delay, guiding me through the detour, and strengthening me through the test.

Today I choose to stand in what You have restored.

I declare faith over fear, obedience over comfort, and purpose over regret. Use my life as evidence that You still resurrect dreams—and that You are faithful to finish what You begin.

I trust You with what's next.

I trust You with who I'm becoming.

In Jesus' name,

Amen.

A Final Word

The Dream Still Lives

If you have walked through these pages honestly, you have probably recognized parts of your own story.

Maybe you saw yourself in the darkness.

Maybe you recognized the waiting.

Maybe the detour felt painfully familiar.

You may have remembered dreams that once felt buried under disappointment, delay, or discouragement. You may have wondered whether certain chapters of your life had quietly closed forever.

But the message of this journey is simple and powerful:

God is not finished.

The same God who carried Joseph out of a pit, the same God who restored the Shunammite woman's son, the same God who rolled the stone away from a borrowed tomb is still writing resurrection stories today.

And your life is one of them.

The dream you thought was over may have only been resting.

The vision you thought was buried may have only been planted.

The season you thought was the end may have only been preparation.

Because when God is involved, endings rarely stay endings.

They become beginnings.

So walk forward with courage.

Trust what God is doing—even when you cannot fully see it yet.

Hold on to hope—even when circumstances feel uncertain.

And when life invites you to believe again, do not hesitate.

Dream again.

Dream boldly.

Dream faithfully.

Dream with the quiet confidence that the Author of your story is still writing.

Because resurrection was never meant to stay in a chapter.

It was meant to become a way of living.

And if God has brought your dream back to life once…

He can do it again.

As long as God is still breathing purpose into you, your dream is never finished.

Afterword

Your Resurrection Blueprint

If you have made it this far, pause for a moment.

Not because the journey is over—but because something has shifted.

Books end.

Journeys do not.

When I began writing *Resurrecting Your Dreams*, my prayer was simple: that these pages would meet someone in the middle of their process. Not after everything was resolved. Not after the dream had already come back to life. But in the middle—where questions linger, where faith stretches, and where hope sometimes feels fragile.

Because that is where most of us live.

We live between promise and fulfillment.

Between prayer and answer.

Between Friday and Sunday.

And yet that middle space is exactly where God does some of His greatest work.

If this book has resonated with you, it is likely because you have seen pieces of your own story along the way. Maybe you recognized yourself in Joseph's pit, where dreams seemed buried beneath betrayal. Maybe you felt the tension of the Shunammite woman, standing between grief and restoration. Maybe you saw your own journey reflected in the waiting, the detours, the stretching, and the quiet seasons where it felt like nothing was happening.

But something was happening.

God was working.

This book was never meant to be read quickly and placed on a shelf. It was meant to be walked through. To sit with you in quiet moments. To meet you in honest reflection. To remind you—again and again—that what God started in you is still alive.

Because resurrection is not a one-time event.

It is a pattern.

The Resurrection Blueprint

Throughout this journey, we have returned again and again to a sacred rhythm:

Friday's Pain → Saturday's Pause → Sunday's Power

This rhythm appears throughout Scripture.

It appears in the lives of biblical dreamers.

And if you are honest, it appears in your life as well.

Friday represents the pain—the loss, the disappointment, the moment when it feels like the dream has died.

Saturday represents the pause—the waiting, the silence, the uncertainty, the space where God is working but not explaining.

Sunday represents the power—the resurrection, the renewal, the moment when God does what only He can do.

This rhythm is not just the story of Easter.

It is the pattern of transformation.

Joseph had a Friday when he was thrown into a pit.

He had a Saturday in prison where the promise seemed delayed.

But he eventually had a Sunday when he stood in purpose before Pharaoh.

The Shunammite woman had a Friday when her son died.

She had a Saturday as she journeyed toward the prophet.

But she had a Sunday when life returned to what had been lost.

Even Jesus walked through this rhythm.

Friday looked like defeat.

Saturday felt like silence.

Sunday revealed resurrection.

But here is the revelation:

You do not move through this rhythm only once.

You will experience many Fridays.

You will endure many Saturdays.

And by God's grace, you will witness many Sundays.

The goal of faith is not to avoid the process.

The goal is to understand it.

Because when you understand the blueprint, you stop panicking in Friday's pain. You stop losing hope in Saturday's silence. You begin trusting that Sunday's power is still on the way.

Living the Blueprint

Once you recognize this pattern, something changes.

You begin to see your life differently.

Moments that once felt like endings begin to look like preparation.

Seasons that once felt confusing begin to reveal purpose.

And the dream that once seemed lost begins to rise again with new clarity.

Because the truth every dreamer eventually learns is this:

The dream is not just about the destination.

It is about the person God shapes along the way.

Sometimes God resurrects the dream by changing the circumstances.

Other times He resurrects the dream by changing the dreamer.

And often the greatest miracle is not simply that the dream returns—but that you are stronger, wiser, and more surrendered when it does.

The Journey Continues

So as you close this book, I want to leave you with a simple encouragement.

Do not rush the process.

Trust the seasons God allows in your life. Trust the waiting. Trust the preparation. Trust the quiet moments when it feels like nothing is happening—because often those are the moments when God is doing the deepest work.

And when the time comes—and it will—step forward with courage.

Dream again.

Dream with humility.

Dream with faith.

Dream with the quiet confidence that the same God who carried you through the dark will also guide you into the light.

Because your story is still unfolding.

And somewhere ahead of you is a moment when you will look back and realize that what once felt like an ending was actually God preparing a resurrection.

Until that day:

Keep trusting.

Keep growing.

Keep believing.

And never forget:

God finishes what He starts.

— Scot C. Moore

About the Author

Scot C. Moore is an author and speaker who helps people navigate life's transitions and rediscover purpose after seasons of change. Drawing from years of leadership and mentoring experience, he blends thoughtful storytelling with practical insight to help readers turn setbacks into clarity, resilience, and renewed momentum — inviting them to move forward with intention and dare to dream again.